DISTANCE LEARNING
for Elementary STEM
Creative Projects for Teachers and Families

Amanda Thomas

International Society for Technology in Education

PORTLAND, OREGON • ARLINGTON, VIRGINIA

Distance Learning for Elementary STEM: Creative Projects for Teachers and Families
Amanda Thomas

Senior Director of Books and Journals: Colin Murcray
Senior Acquisitions Editor: Valerie Witte
Content Contributor: Courtney Burkholder
Copyeditor: Joanna Szabo
Proofreader: Linda Laflamme
Indexer: Valerie Haynes Perry
Book Design and Production: Kim McGovern
Cover Design: Beth DeWilde

Library of Congress Cataloging-in-Publication Data
Names: Thomas, Amanda (Math professor), author.
Title: Distance learning for elementary STEM : creative projects for teachers and families / Amanda Thomas.
Description: First edition. | Portland, Oregon : International Society for Technology in Education, 2020. | Includes bibliographical references and index.
Identifiers: LCCN 2020035072 (print) | LCCN 2020035073 (ebook) | ISBN 9781564848710 (paperback) | ISBN 9781564848680 (epub) | ISBN 9781564848697 (mobi) | ISBN 9781564848703 (pdf)
Subjects: LCSH: Science—Study and teaching (Elementary)—Activity programs. | Mathematics—Study and teaching (Elementary)—Activity programs. | Science—Web-based instruction. | Mathematics—Web-based instruction.
Classification: LCC LB1585 .T55 2020 (print) | LCC LB1585 (ebook) | DDC 372.35/044—dc23
LC record available at https://lccn.loc.gov/2020035072
LC ebook record available at https://lccn.loc.gov/2020035073

First Edition
ISBN: 978-1-56484-871-0
Ebook version available

Printed in the United States of America

ISTE® is a registered trademark of the International Society for Technology in Education.

About ISTE

The International Society for Technology in Education (ISTE) is a nonprofit organization that works with the global education community to accelerate the use of technology to solve tough problems and inspire innovation. Our worldwide network believes in the potential technology holds to transform teaching and learning.

ISTE sets a bold vision for education transformation through the ISTE Standards, a framework for students, educators, administrators, coaches and computer science educators to rethink education and create innovative learning environments. ISTE hosts the annual ISTE Conference & Expo, one of the world's most influential edtech events. The organization's professional learning offerings include online courses, professional networks, year-round academies, peer-reviewed journals and other publications. ISTE is also the leading publisher of books focused on technology in education. For more information or to become an ISTE member, visit iste.org. Subscribe to ISTE's YouTube channel and connect with ISTE on Twitter, Facebook and LinkedIn.

Related ISTE Titles

STEAM Power: Infusing Art Into Your STEM Curriculum, by Tim Needles

The Perfect Blend: A Practical Guide to Designing Student-Centered Learning Experiences, by Michele Eaton

Building a K–12 STEM Lab: A Step-by-Step Guide for School Leaders and Tech Coaches, by Deborah Nagler and Martha Osei-Yaw

About the Author

Amanda Thomas, Ph.D., is an assistant professor of mathematics education in the Department of Teaching, Learning, and Teacher Education at University of Nebraska–Lincoln. She received her doctoral degree in 2013 from the University of Missouri–Columbia. Her research focuses on teachers' use of mobile technology in elementary mathematics classrooms. She's also interested in STEM education and supporting teachers in innovative STEM integration.

Publisher's Acknowledgments

ISTE gratefully acknowledges the contributions of the following:

ISTE Standards Reviewers

Jeff Dungan

Kelly Grogan

Dominic Hill

Julie Sessions

Manuscript Reviewers

Kelly Bornmann

Janine Feil

Karey Killian

Krishna Millsapp

Jessica Shupik

Dedication

To all the families and educators who persevered and innovated throughout the COVID-19 pandemic.

Contents

Introduction

Elementary children experience the world through play, and they learn best when actively engaged in hands-on content learning, often with peers. But in the spring of 2020, teachers and families throughout the world grappled with how to keep young children engaged in learning while isolated at home during a pandemic. Educators were suddenly faced with designing emergency distance instruction for children of all ages, with unequal access to technology and high-speed internet, usually with minimal experience with online learning.

At the same time, parents were thrust into new roles as homeschool teachers, often while adapting to job loss or working from home themselves. Teachers, administrators, academics, professional organizations, and edtech companies sprang into action, offering a variety of supports and resources for teachers and students to teach and learn online. Meanwhile, families supported young children's distance learning at home as best they could under extraordinary circumstances. Yet, few easily accessible, high-quality resources provided support for both teachers and parents to support engaging, distance STEM learning for elementary children.

The flexibility of online schooling offers an unprecedented chance to engage children in active learning through project-based STEM experiences. As the saying goes, with great challenges come great opportunities. Widespread distance learning at the elementary level is challenging for many educators and families, but it also permits innovation and individualization that can be difficult in traditional school settings. Research and practice have long indicated the positive potential of contextualized, integrated teaching approaches; yet standards, class time, lessons, textbooks, and assessments remain overwhelmingly siloed into individual subject areas.

About the Book

K–5 teachers can use this book to inform their design of distance STEM education. Families can use the STEM projects in this book to supplement and enrich their child's school-based distance learning at home.

This book offers a collection of elementary STEM projects that educators and families can adapt to individual children's needs and interests as part of distance learning.

The first chapter addresses supports for educators designing distance STEM learning for elementary children, and speaks to parents', families', and caregivers' perspectives about STEM learning for young children.

The next eight chapters feature STEM projects designed around themes, aligned to STEM content standards for grades K through 5, and adaptable for flexible online and offline use. Technology resources—which might include videos, applets, or online games—are used to launch each project. The chapters include activities related to science and math as well as engineering challenges. The engineering component introduces children to a type of engineering that corresponds with the theme of the chapter. Engineering design challenges them to extend learning about the project theme so that STEM learning is applied and connected in engaging, hands-on experiences.

This book concludes with suggestions and guidelines for teachers and families to design their own creative STEM projects that can keep children engaged in rich, fun learning experiences.

Supporting Distance STEM Learning for Elementary Children

The elementary STEM projects in this book are designed for distance, online, blended, and remote learning. These projects are not curriculum materials akin to textbooks or lesson plans. Instead, each project is an adaptable set of ideas, designed around a central theme. Teachers and families can choose the components that best align with their students' grade levels and draw from other options for enrichment or remediation activities.

STEM Projects Overview

This section provides a breakdown of the components of each project-based chapter, which includes connections to relevant standards and grade-level guidelines, with suggestions for students in grades K–2 and 3–5. Each project provides information on necessary materials; suggested online resources; and extensions and connections beyond STEM, such as film, literature, and fine arts.

Connection to Standards

All projects in this book are aligned to standards that connect with the four STEM content areas: science, technology, engineering, and mathematics. Standards help articulate expectations for student learning, and alignment with standards helps ensure that students learn content they're "supposed to know" in an order and depth that is developmentally appropriate.

The standards to which activities in this book are aligned are all widely adopted in the US and informed by decades of research and practice in STEM education content areas. However, some states have adopted their own standards, often heavily influenced by the ISTE Standards, Next Generation Science Standards (NGSS), and Common Core State Standards for Mathematics (CCSSM) (Pruitt, 2014; Reys, et al., 2013). While exact alignment to state-level standards may differ, big ideas tend to be somewhat consistent (Thomas & Edson, 2014) and children who engage in these activities will learn STEM content that is useful no matter where they are. Families may have a variety of perspectives and questions about standards, but it is important to keep in mind that they are all goals for learning designed to prepare children for eventual success in college and careers. Emphasis on standards throughout this book is intended to reassure educators and families that the STEM projects align with what children are expected to learn in school.

Table 1.1 provides access to key sources for standards that are addressed in the book.

TABLE 1.1 STEM Content Standards and Related Resources

Next Generation Science Standards (NGSS)	
NGSS Parent Guides	
Common Core State Standards for Mathematics (CCSSM)	
CCSSM What Parents Should Know	
NASA Definition of Engineering	
Engineering Design Process from NASA	
ISTE Standards for Students	

ISTE Standards for Students

In each of the project chapters, technology connections are aligned to ISTE Standards for Students, which are "designed to empower student voice and ensure that learning is a student-driven process." Teachers and families can and should also draw upon their own creativity and the technologies they are comfortable using in their distance schooling contexts to provide options for assessing students' work in a variety of ways. In doing so, children may also have opportunities to develop understanding of additional ISTE Standards for Students (scan the QR code in Table 1.1 to view the Standards in full).

Next Generation Science Standards (NGSS)

Exploratory Science activities for each chapter are aligned with the Next Generation Science Standards (NGSS). The NGSS standards that are identified for each project are grade-level performance expectations. Some projects include standards from every grade, but all include one or more standards from each grade range, or "band" (K–2 or 3–5). And while activities generally support three-dimensional learning as promoted in NGSS, these dimensions are not explicitly stated within the chapters.

Each STEM project chapter culminates in engineering projects that apply a combination of math, science, and technology learning. These projects are aligned to specific Engineering Design performance expectations in NGSS and incorporate the engineering design process and engineering habits of mind.

Common Core State Standards for Mathematics (CCSSM)

Math activities are aligned with Common Core State Standards for Mathematics and organized in K–2 and 3–5 grade bands. Grade-level content standards are identified, but activities are also mindful of the eight CCSSM mathematical practices in Table 1.2 that describe habits of mind for mathematical learners. Math activities encourage reasoning and sense-making, with intended balance between conceptual understanding and procedural fluency (NCTM, 2014).

TABLE 1.2 CCSSM Standards for Mathematical Practice (CCSSI & NGA, 2010)

MP1. Make sense of problems and persevere in solving them.

MP2. Reason abstractly and quantitatively.

MP3. Construct viable arguments and critique the reasoning of others.

MP4. Model with mathematics.

MP5. Use appropriate tools strategically.

MP6. Attend to precision.

MP7. Look for and make use of structure.

MP8. Look for and express regularity in repeated reasoning.

Materials, Time, and Supervision

In each chapter, you will find an overview and description of what is needed for the activities. While access to a connected device is assumed for online learning activities, each project offers a menu of possibilities involving many options for resources. To the greatest extent possible, materials include items that many families may have available at home with occasional options for more specialized STEM materials and toys. A single project can include options ranging from toilet paper rolls, old boxes, and tape, to toys or robots that some kids may have access to outside of school.

Even during online schooling, active, engaging, hands-on experiences are essential for young children's learning. Therefore, each chapter offers offline possibilities that children can do at home with a variety of resources. To make the activities more customizable and accessible to populations of students with inequitable access to materials, many options are offered. An elementary teacher might select some activities to incorporate directly in a distance class and include others as optional activities for families to do together. Encouraging offline activities is highly recommended, as these tend to be hands-on activities that can "hook" students into the content of the lesson, while also helping bridge a digital divide.

Resources to Explore and Inspire

A mix of digital and physical activities with a variety of options allows you to customize learning experiences in ways that work best for individual students and families. Therefore, project activities incorporate a blend of dynamic digital options (e.g., videos, websites, applets) and ideas that can be embedded within an online learning management system (e.g., downloadable worksheet ideas, questions, and prompts).

Although each chapter identifies useful technology resources prior to science, mathematics, and engineering activities, technology need not come first. In some cases, a short video or game might be used to help establish the context for the rest of the activities, but with other resources, it may make more sense to incorporate technology at a later point in the activities. For example, resources that are incorporated within a science lesson that follows the Engage-Explore-Explain-Elaborate-Evaluate format might include more of the technology resources in the Explain phase of the lesson to support children in relating their own observations to science concepts (Duran & Duran, 2004).

Grade-Level Guidelines

Projects in this book are designed for elementary children in kindergarten through grade 5. Of course, there are major differences between what children in primary grades are expected to learn and expectations for children in intermediate grades. Each chapter highlights how the projects align with math and science standards for two grade bands, grades K–2 and grades 3–5. Suggestions are offered for younger children, sometimes for specific grade levels in relation to standards. Engineering activities identify standards for K–2 and 3–5, but the activities are flexible enough to span across grade levels in most cases. A benefit of distance learning is the flexibility to adapt to the needs, background knowledge, and interests of individual children. Grade band suggestions are intended as a guide, but each project can also be customized to create learning experiences that meet the needs of individual children.

Extensions and Connections

Each chapter concludes with ideas for extending and connecting thematic STEM learning with other areas and disciplines, such as entertainment, children's literature, writing, social studies, and fine arts. While standards for these content areas exist, they are beyond the scope of this book. Extensions to other content areas tend to be more general than STEM connections, and educators may wish to align content connections more specifically or identify them as options for children to further pursue topics that are of particular interest.

How Educators Can Support Distance STEM Learning

Most elementary teachers are accustomed to planning for physical classroom environments, routines, interactions, and teaching. And while teaching and managing a room full of young children requires a great deal of skill and compassion, teaching practices for online learning may seem even more daunting. How can virtual environments possibly support the learning needs of children who developmentally rely on concrete experiences and emotionally need affirming teacher–student relationships? The truth is that online learning will not replicate in-person experiences, especially for elementary-age children. Online teaching isn't better or worse; it's just different—and it can be difficult, especially when it is new or rushed. This section describes considerations for elementary teachers to design and support online STEM learning, as well as information for teachers to implement the projects in Chapters 2–9.

Ensuring Equitable Learning

Unlike middle school, high school, or college students, elementary children are rarely alone when they engage in online learning. In most cases, younger children participate in online schooling while under the supervision of a parent, older sibling, or caregiver. On the one hand, this is a great opportunity to partner with families and caregivers in a very direct way. On the other hand, families and caregivers must take on heavier responsibilities for supporting young children's online schooling. Some families may be better positioned to embrace those responsibilities, while others may face greater challenges. Just as in the classroom, it is of the utmost importance for distance elementary teachers to know the children and their families when planning for instruction. The better relationships teachers can develop with children and their parents, the better they can understand the opportunities and constraints students and families face with online learning.

One of the biggest challenges for distance learning is planning for equitable learning in situations that may be quite inequitable for children (Rose, 2014). Often online learning is designed for children who speak the predominant language and reside in middle-class households with access to high-speed internet, a computer, safe and quiet spaces to work, and a stay-at-home parent. This approach does not acknowledge the diverse cultures, experiences, needs, and circumstances of all children. These issues transcend individual teachers and are often made at the administrative level. Those who teach elementary children online must consider and plan for a wide variety of issues, including many they may be unable to solve. These considerations include such things as:

- Does each child have the computing technology and bandwidth necessary for this lesson?

- What experiences do children and families have with the technology used to facilitate distance schooling?

- Are distance schooling resources accessible to children and families whose first language is not English?

- When are children engaging in distance schooling (not all families' work schedules are conducive to typical school days and times)?

- How does distance schooling support learners with special needs?

- How can children and families seek distance schooling support or ask questions?

- Because schools provide so much more than academics, is each child safe and are their basic needs being met?

Answers to some of these questions are easier than others, and most extend well beyond an individual teacher. But all elementary educators can and must acknowledge children's diverse identities and circumstances when designing and implementing online schooling. Flexibility, communication, creativity, and grace are essential. The activities in this book incorporate flexibility to more equitably meet the needs of every student and family.

Elementary teachers can pick and choose among STEM activities and adapt them for the needs of their students in a distance setting—or for the classroom, too! While potential alignments with content standards are highlighted in each chapter, teachers may find ways to delve deeper into understanding given standards or may recognize connections to other standards. Activities and alignments are suggestions to build upon and invite teachers' specialized knowledge to best align with learning expectations and children's needs.

Ideas for Assessment

One question that may linger for many teachers is how to assess student learning within these projects. Some activities suggest tables or worksheets that can be completed and submitted like any other work in an online course. Some activities include experiences that are not as easy to "turn in" or assess. Teachers are encouraged to take advantage of technology for these types of activities. For instance, have students take and share photos of drawings or engineering design projects, or have classes incorporate a tool such as Flipgrid to easily create and share short videos of students' experiences or their reflections about what they learned in a project. Alternatively, have students create videos or screencasts to share in approved educational spaces such as Google Classroom or Edmodo; demonstrate their learning through creating and sharing presentations, slide decks, or written work; or communicate with other students in a discussion board. These are general suggestions that span across activities. Some specific suggestions are included within activities, but educators can apply a variety of technologies to assess student learning in ways that connect with their teaching practices.

Possibilities abound, but educators must be mindful of the diverse circumstances for distance learning, as well as what is developmentally appropriate for young learners. Activities include ideas and resources to support teachers in this work, but choose flexibility over a prescriptive approach. Teachers can and should also draw upon their own creativity and the technologies they are comfortable using in their distance schooling contexts to provide options for assessing students' work in a variety of ways.

How Families Can Support Distance STEM learning

Throughout April 2020, the United Nations Educational, Scientific and Cultural Organization (UNESCO) reported that more than 90% of the world's children had been impacted by school closures due to COVID-19. Never in modern history had distance and remote learning been implemented at this scale. Unsurprisingly, adapting to schooling at home was a challenge for many families. As parents began abruptly shifting to homeschooling their children, social media was quickly flooded with posts and memes, humorously but sincerely affirming how invaluable teachers truly are. As teachers and schools rallied to rapidly shift to new modes of learning, families were the ones responsible for motivating, supervising, and holding children accountable for learning—from home—during a traumatic time in world history.

In many households with elementary children (including my own), emergency online schooling resulted in frequent struggles to get kids to do their schoolwork, stay on task, and learn enough to minimize disruptions to their education. Most families know it's not as easy as asking a young child to log on to their online class at 8:00 a.m. and work independently until they've completed their lessons and schoolwork.

There are plenty of reasons why online schooling for elementary children during a global pandemic is challenging for kids and families, many of which relate to the equity considerations identified earlier in this chapter. And while many of those reasons are beyond our control, we can address what we know about children's learning. By and large, children learn best when they are actively engaged in interesting content that provides opportunities for three Cs: communication, collaboration, and connections (O'Connell & Groom, 2010). In the best of circumstances, these opportunities can be difficult to create in distance classes (or physical classrooms, for that matter).

Teachers spend years acquiring the professional education and expertise needed to design engaging lessons and facilitate active learning that meets the diverse needs of every student in their classrooms, so it's no wonder that keeping children actively and independently engaged in distance learning for hours each day is challenging for many families. But, for many kids, staying engaged in a video game for hours on end seems easy and is often the reason that families impose limits on screen time. This book offers some possibilities for how we can harness that type of online engagement, combined with hands-on activities at home, to motivate STEM learning for elementary children.

An Integrated Approach

The STEM projects in this book provide children with opportunities to learn grade-appropriate math and science through a variety of activities centered around a particular theme. By using an integrated, project-based STEM learning approach, children can delve more deeply into a topic over the course of a week or two, exploring and applying what they learn about science, technology, engineering, and math in active, engaging ways. And while many of the activities should be fun and may feel like play to children, parents and families can feel confident that they are still learning what they "need to know," because each project is aligned to grade-level math and science standards (Common Core State Standards for Mathematics and Next Generation Science Standards, respectively). Projects include ideas for connecting to other content areas outside of STEM, as well.

Chapters 2–9 also include support for families to make sense of the integrated support, content standards, and suggested strategies. Maybe you've seen some version of an online meme that reads something like: "Kids learning Common Core are about to learn how to carry the one from their homeschool teacher." Contemporary standards, such as Common Core, and the approaches teachers use to teach those standards are unfamiliar and may seem unnecessarily complicated to many parents and families. But while it might seem easier and more familiar for adults to immediately jump to procedures like "carry the one," there are solid, research-based reasons why kids learn a variety of strategies (and most of those strategies eventually lead to strategies and algorithms that are familiar to parents anyway). When appropriate, the activities in this book describe strategies that families might find unfamiliar and explain why those strategies are valuable for children's learning.

How to Apply What You Learn

In order to facilitate online STEM learning with the projects in this book, parents and families do not need to be education or STEM experts, but chapters do provide helpful insights for navigating this new learning experience with emphasis on essential standards, children's needs, and a solid STEM foundation. Tips and explanations highlight background and reasoning for activities. Many of the technology resources also offer background and content knowledge families may find valuable. Each chapter includes questions and discussion prompts that can help families communicate about STEM learning. Families might consider using these prompts to initiate STEM discussions at dinner or while on a walk. Not only can these discussions offer more conversation than what often results from the standard "What did you learn in school today?" but responding to purposeful questions and discussion prompts allows children to learn more by communicating their thinking out loud with you (Mercer et al., 2004; Sfard, 2001).

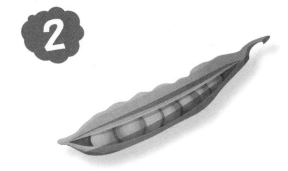

How Does Your Garden Grow?

In this STEM project, children will learn about science, technology, engineering, and math through exploring plant growth. The chapter leads with the relevant ISTE Standards for Students and a description of materials, time, and supervision needed for the activities in the chapter. Technology resources and science, mathematics, and engineering activities focused on plant growth follow, along with connections to NGSS and Common Core State Standards for Mathematics. At the end of the chapter, you'll find plant-themed ideas to extend and support learning about children's literature, social studies, art, and media connections.

ISTE Standards for Students

Overall, the uses of technology in this chapter are most aligned with the following ISTE Standards for Students. Technology learning opportunities can be expanded by asking children to share their learning through a variety of tools (e.g., discussion boards, slide decks, or videos of their own).

Empowered Learner

1c. Students use technology to seek feedback that informs and improves their practice and to demonstrate their learning in a variety of ways.

Knowledge Constructor

3d. Students build knowledge by actively exploring real-world issues and problems, developing ideas and theories and pursuing answers and solutions.

Innovative Designer

4d. Students exhibit a tolerance for ambiguity, perseverance and the capacity to work with open-ended problems.

Materials, Time, and Supervision

This unit draws upon a number of online and offline resources. However, it is not necessary for families to make a trip to their local garden center—there are options for growing plants from kitchen scraps and other readily available resources. Backyard or community gardens and farms are excellent resources to draw upon for this chapter.

TABLE 2.1 Project Materials

REQUIRED	OPTIONAL
• A connected device with high-speed internet for plant growth simulations, apps, and some of the games	• Access to video games, movies, and robotics resources • Access to sunlight, soil, and water • Seeds or plants to grow • Long tube (empty paper towel or gift wrap cardboard tube)

Most children should spend a total of 10–20 hours on the activities in this project, or between 2–3 hours a day for a week or two, with plant growing activities extending longer depending on the specific plants. There is a balance between work that children can complete relatively independently, activities that may require more adult guidance, and prompts to engage in discussion around STEM ideas. Some children, especially early readers, will need oral directions to get started with the activities you select. Safety considerations for the activities in this chapter include handwashing after handling soil and seeds, supervision and reminders not to taste plants or scraps, and guidance with the tools needed to create the engineering design project at the end of the chapter.

Resources to Explore and Inspire

Various technologies can be used to establish the context of plant growth for this project and to support the content throughout. Depending on the particular video or child, these resources can be used to launch the collection of activities, formulate questions, or pique general curiosity that leads to the more specific activities throughout this chapter. The resources in Table 2.2 can also be used to help children explain and connect their real-world exploration and observations with more formal science content.

TABLE 2.2 Resources to Explore: How Does Your Garden Grow?

RESOURCE	DESCRIPTION	GRADE LEVEL	CODE
PBS Learning Media: From Seed to Fruit	Young children can explore the stages of plant growth in the From Seed to Fruit interactive from PBS.	K–1	qrgo.page.link/hjZgX
PBS Kids: Planting a Seed	PBS Kids short video clip about planting a seed, along with investigation suggestions from Sid the Science Kid.	K–2	qrgo.page.link/CtdF7

(Continued)

RESOURCE	DESCRIPTION	GRADE LEVEL	CODE
The Generation Genius: Plant Growth Conditions	Video, discussion questions, activity guide, and lesson materials focused on conditions for plant growth.	K–2	qrgo.page.link/iKT9F
The Generation Genius: Plants Need Water and Light	Video, discussion questions, activity guide, and lesson materials focused on plants needing water and light.	K–2	qrgo.page.link/jwnMu
Bill Nye the Science Guy: Bill Nye Plants	This full-length Bill Nye video explains how plants grow and their importance for humans. (*Note:* this video requires a sign-in to access.)	3–5	bit.ly/3fk6y8Q
The Generation Genius: Animal & Plant Life Cycles	Video, discussion questions, activity guide, and lesson materials focused on animal and plant life cycles.	3–5	qrgo.page.link/u9216
University of Illinois Extension: The Great Plant Escape	Older students can investigate plant life through Great Plant Escape cases.	4–5	qrgo.page.link/2vMvi

Your community or curriculum may provide other technology-based learning opportunities about plant growth; the ones provided here are simply examples of the ways in which technology can be used to support learning around the theme of plant growth. Technology learning opportunities can be expanded by asking children to create their own slide decks or videos and share their learning through a variety of tools (e.g., discussion boards, presentations).

Science: Growing a Plant

What is a project about plant growth without an opportunity to grow some plants? To support science learning, children will grow their own plants and investigate what plants need to survive and how they grow.

NGSS Disciplinary Core Ideas for Science

Science learning in this chapter aligns with the standards shown here. The standards emphasize communicating about science, including concepts such as *describe, construct an argument,* and *support an argument.* Thus, it is especially important that children have opportunities to communicate their scientific thinking either in writing or in discussion with teachers, peers, or family members.

K-2 ACTIVITIES	3-5 ACTIVITIES
K-LS1-1. Use observations to describe patterns of what plants and animals (including humans) need to survive. **2-LS2-1.** Plan and conduct an investigation to determine if plants need sunlight and water to grow.	**4-LS1-1.** Construct an argument that plants and animals have internal and external structures that function to support survival, growth, behavior, and reproduction. **5-LS1-1.** Support an argument that plants get the materials they need for growth chiefly from air and water.

Getting Started

Begin with growing the plant. The details of this exploration will depend somewhat on which seeds or starter plants kids can access. If children have access to seeds, good choices will be those that germinate quickly, such as radishes, watermelons, squash, peas, beans, or quick-growing flowers like marigolds or zinnias.

Keep in mind that some seeds are very small and may be difficult for young children to handle.

If children don't have easy access to seeds for this project, they can use kitchen scraps! A quick Google search of "growing plants from scraps" will yield a number of specific suggestions. Regrowing plants from kitchen scraps will require some shifts in discussions since children won't be growing a plant from a seed. But the same important concepts can be addressed. Vegetables with roots such as celery, onions, or lettuces can be regrown in soil or just water, providing perhaps an even better illustration that plants get the materials they need for growth primarily from air and water (NGSS 5-LS1-1). Figures 2.1 and 2.2 illustrate plants growing from kitchen scraps.

Figure 2.1 Replanted celery grows in soil.

Figure 2.2 An onion regrows in water.

At home, children can grow their plants using materials they have available. A paper cup, a bowl, an empty egg carton, or empty toilet paper rolls cut in half and placed on a plate are all affordable options for plant containers. Figure 2.3 shows a child growing a seed in a Styrofoam cup. And while high-quality soil can result in speedier, healthier plant growth, children can use whatever soil is available to them and consider that to be part of their investigation.

Figure 2.3 A child waters a seed she has planted in a cup.

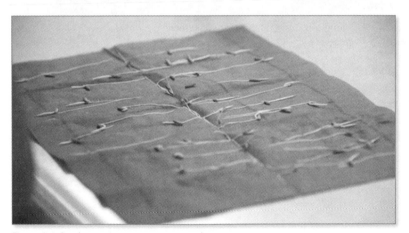

Figure 2.4 Seeds germinate on a paper towel.

Students can also sprout seeds and watch the full germination of a seed by placing the seeds in a moistened paper towel, placing the towel in a plastic bag, and taping the bag to a window. The resulting sprout might resemble Figure 2.4.

Grade-Level Guidelines

It is important to help children connect the activity of growing plants with the scientific ideas they should learn and understand. One approach can be to ask children to keep a journal. This could be in a paper notebook or an online journal using a shared Google Doc, slides, blogs, or vlogs. The journal might begin with observations about the seed—what do they notice? What do they wonder? Older children might use digital resources or a book to learn about parts of a seed to draw and label. Ask children to make predictions and document what they notice as their plants grow. They should also record important data about the growing conditions to help them interpret any patterns they notice. Figure 2.5 is an example of what an observation journal could look like for one plant. The language and units of measurement should be adapted to meet the needs of younger learners. Students might also include measurement data of plant heights over time. Alternatively, children could draw pictures each day to document their observations.

PLANT GROWTH JOURNAL

Plant Type: Bean

Plant Location: Windowsill

Day	Water (spoonfuls)	Sunlight (hours of sun)	What do you notice?
1	1	4	It is cloudy outside.
2	1	6	The dirt was dry before watering
...	...	...	...
7	1	6	I can see the plant growing!

Figure 2.5 Students can record observations of plant growth in a journal.

Grades K–2

At the K–2 level, science standards indicate that children should be focusing on patterns of what plants need to survive and investigating whether plants need sunlight and water to grow. This can be accomplished in the simple experiment described below.

- Children plant three similar seeds or scraps:

  - Place one in sunlight with no water.

  - Place another with no sunlight, but water appropriately.

  - Place the third plant in sunlight and water regularly.

- If other conditions are held relatively constant, students should observe that the plant grown with sunlight and water flourishes more than the others.

- Encourage and guide the child to plan their own experiments to see how the amount of water or time in sunlight impacts their plant.

Especially with very young children, adults should help monitor plant conditions such as planting in appropriately sized containers or including a good amount of soil and water to begin with so that initial planting conditions do not completely shut down the phenomenon children are trying to explore. For instance, consistent overwatering may not help children discover that water is needed for plant growth because it could have the opposite effect of killing the plant. Similarly, if a child places a seed at the bottom of a deep cup and covers the entire thing with several inches of soil, the planting conditions may impede the realization that sunlight helps plants grow. While parents and teachers may want to avoid situations that are doomed from the start, there is also value in allowing children enough room for exploration that they can learn these important phenomena for themselves. The personalized nature of distance learning may help adults find the balance between productive failure and frustration that can shut down learning.

Grades 3–5

Plant growth experiments with children in upper elementary grades can be quite similar to those for younger children, but with additional focus on the function of plant structures and where plants get the materials needed for growth. The plant growth activity could be combined with curriculum-based assignments to identify parts of plants and their functions, as shown in Figure 2.6.

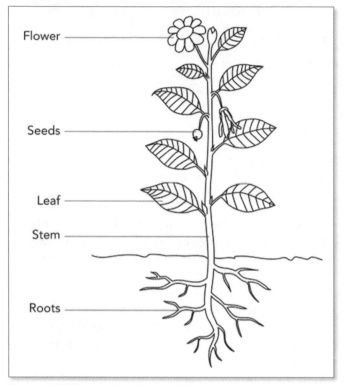

Flower

Seeds

Leaf

Stem

Roots

Figure 2.6 Children can label diagrams of plant parts.

To emphasize student thinking about where plants get materials needed for growth and connect more traditional tasks with hands-on explorations, ask children a number of "Where is/are…", "What do you think…", and "Why do you think…" questions. For instance:

- Where are the roots on your flower?

- What do you think the stem of your bean plant does?

- Why do you think pumpkin plants grow flowers before they grow actual pumpkins?

Emphasizing these types of questions draws attention to the specific scientific content children are expected to learn in grade 4 science standards (e.g., plant structures and functions and materials needed for growth). It is also developmentally appropriate to ask these types of questions to younger children to develop understanding of plant biology from an early age and connect with grades 1 and 2 standards about what plants need to survive. But what about the answers to those questions? To connect the real-world activity with family discussion and online learning, use online tools or connect with curriculum resources to figure out the answers to these questions and compare them to what children predicted or reasoned on their own. Online tools can support the plant growth activity in a variety of ways, as described in Table 2.3.

TABLE 2.3 Technology Resources for Growing a Plant Activities

RESOURCE	DESCRIPTION	GRADE LEVEL	CODE
Mobile Montessori: Parts of Plants	Parts of Plant app includes plant parts and names with botany puzzles.	K–2	qrgo.page.link/PWE52
Appalachian Mountain Club	Photograph flowers and fruits during a hike on the Appalachian Trail.	K–5	qrgo.page.link/sX6nv
Budburst, Chicago Botanic Garden	A collection of citizen science activities for children of all ages to observe and report their observations.	K–5	qrgo.page.link/hj73a
Explore Learning Growing Plants Gizmo	Online plant growth simulator and student activity sheet.	3–5	qrgo.page.link/HWSpX

Math: Plants in a Row

The mathematics in this project emphasizes strategies for adding, subtracting, multiplying, and dividing. Once the context and science of plant growth are well-established, children can use garden arrangements to solve addition and multiplication problems with ten frames and arrays. Educators and families may notice that these activities emphasize strategies and representations that provide a conceptual foundation for fluently adding and multiplying later on. This means that the strategies might not be as easy or familiar, but they do serve an important purpose in helping students learn mathematics with the depth of understanding that allows for fact fluency and flexible application.

Getting Started

Ten frames are a representation that help students visualize quantities in relation to ten, an important benchmark number in the base-ten number system. Chances are, when you mentally add something like 29 + 4 or 58 + 6, you might use benchmarks without realizing it. Mathematically, 29 + 4 is often solved by first decomposing 4 into 3 + 1, thinking of the problem as 29 + 3 + 1, then using the commutative property to change the order to 29 + 1 + 3, the associative property to make a multiple of ten (29 + 1) + 3, and then simplifying 30 + 3 = 33. What might sound and look mathematically complex is a strategy many quickly do in their heads, almost automatically. These ten frames help children develop some of the same basic ways of thinking, developing understanding that will eventually contribute to fact fluency.

Children can use virtual ten frames to represent and solve addition and subtraction problems such as those included in the next section. However, to connect with the garden and plant theme, children in younger grades might start with printouts or downloads of blank ten frames and draw pictures of flowers, leaves, or other plants to model problems on ten frames, to model story problems and/or match equations. Alternatively, students could use small cutouts or stickers of plants or flowers to represent gardens using ten frames. This activity can also be reversed, where ten frame representations are provided and children write corresponding equations and/or word problems. The following example combines two colors of flowers. Be mindful that many children, especially boys, have color blindness, so different types of plants that do not rely on color might be a better option for some children (Xie et al., 2014).

A number of virtual ten frames exist online and can be used to support this activity; scan the QR codes to explore examples.

Didax Virtual Ten Frames

Math Learning Center Virtual Ten Frames

National Council of Teachers of Mathematics (NCTM) Virtual Ten Frames

CCSSM Math Content Standards

The mathematics in this project emphasizes strategies for the basic operations (addition, subtraction, multiplication, and division). Math activities in this project support math standards in K–5, as shown here.

K–2 ACTIVITIES	3–5 ACTIVITIES
CCSS.MATH.CONTENT.K.OA.A.4 For any number from 1 to 9, find the number that makes 10 when added to the given number, e.g., by using objects or drawings, and record the answer with a drawing or equation.	**CCSS.MATH.CONTENT.3.OA.A.1** Interpret products of whole numbers, e.g., interpret 5×7 as the total number of objects in 5 groups of 7 objects each. For example, describe a context in which a total number of objects can be expressed as 5×7.
CCSS.MATH.CONTENT.1.OA.A.2 Solve word problems that call for addition of three whole numbers whose sum is less than or equal to 20, e.g., by using objects, drawings, and equations with a symbol for the unknown number to represent the problem.	**CCSS.MATH.CONTENT.3.OA.A.3** Use multiplication and division within 100 to solve word problems in situations involving equal groups, arrays, and measurement quantities, e.g., by using drawings and equations with a symbol for the unknown number to represent the problem.
CCSS.MATH.CONTENT.2.OA.C.4 Use addition to find the total number of objects arranged in rectangular arrays with up to 5 rows and up to 5 columns; write an equation to express the total as a sum of equal addends.	**CCSS.MATH.CONTENT.4.OA.B.4** Find all factor pairs for a whole number in the range 1-100. Recognize that a whole number is a multiple of each of its factors. Determine whether a given whole number in the range 1–100 is a multiple of a given one-digit number. Determine whether a given whole number in the range 1–100 is prime or composite.

Grade-Level Guidelines

The mathematical ideas in this activity are scaffolded according to grade-level standards. Students progress through representing and solving addition, subtraction, multiplication, and division problems using a variety of strategies. The activities in this chapter are grouped according to K–2 and 3–5 grade bands.

Grades K–2

In kindergarten, children start learning to add one-digit numbers. Beginning in first grade, children are expected to add three one-digit numbers. You can use multiple ten frames and two or three types of plants to pose questions that support these expectations, as shown in Figure 2.7.

Alexandria plants four red flowers and three purple flowers in her garden. Use the ten frame and write an equation to show how many flowers she planted.

$$4 + 3 = 7$$

The ten frame shows some radishes and beans in Alexandria's garden. Write and solve an equation that represents how many plants Alexandria has in her garden.

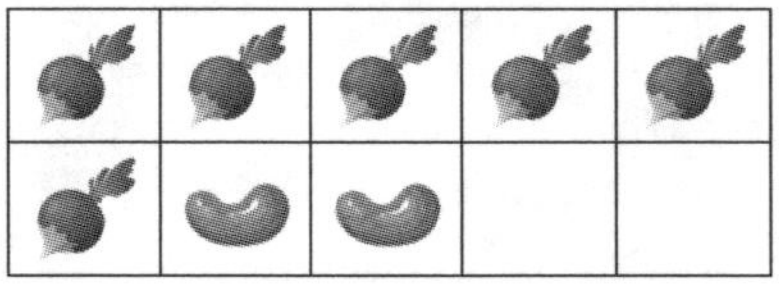

$$6 + 2 = 8$$

In her garden, Katie is growing 5 carrot plants, 4 tomato plants, and 6 pepper plants in her garden. Use the ten frame to show how many plants are in Katie's garden and write an equation.

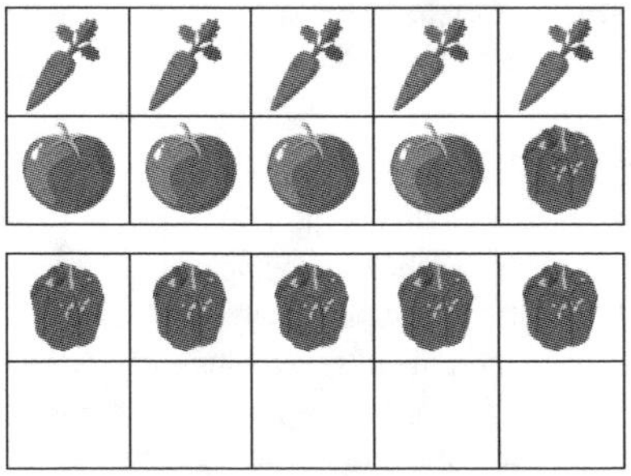

$$5 + 4 + 6 = 15$$

Figure 2.7 Grade 1 students can use ten frames to represent and solve addition problems.

In grade 2, adding with arrays and skip counting helps lay the groundwork for multiplication in grade 3. While ten frames are often no longer necessary, students continue to use visual representations to make sense of mathematical ideas. Within the context of plants and gardens, math problems can focus on up to 5 rows, each with up to 5 plants. For instance, Frank grew 4 rows of corn with 5 stalks in each row. How many corn plants did Frank grow? At this stage, students might count plants, one by one, in their array picture, skip count, or use a series of addition problems (e.g., $5 + 5 + 5 + 5$ or $5 + 5 = 10$, $10 + 5 = 15$, and $15 + 5 = 20$, or $5 + 5 = 10$, $5 + 5 = 10$, $10 + 10 = 20$).

Grades 3–5

By grade 3, students should connect arrays to multiplication, writing equations such as $5 \times 5 = 25$ to represent 5 rows of 5 corn stalks. They should also begin working with arrays with up to 10 or 12 columns and rows of plants as they develop understanding that will lead to fluency with basic multiplication facts. In grades 3–5, kids can also use arrays and inverse relationships to learn about division and factors in the context of plants and gardens. Figure 2.8 illustrates possible tasks that support mathematics learning for grades 2–5.

Write and solve an equation to match the picture of corn stalks planted in Alonzo's garden.

Adaptations: Specify whether children should write an addition, multiplication, or division equation. Or, ask children to write and solve as many equations as they can to match the figure.

Lola has 35 tomato seedlings to plant in her vegetable garden and wants each row to have the same number of tomato plants. Can she plant the tomato plants in 6 rows? Why or why not? Draw some pictures showing how Lola could plant her tomatoes.

Figure 2.8 In grades 3–5 students can use arrays for addition and multiplication and inverse operations.

Online games can reinforce the math that students learn in this project. Table 2.4 summarizes some interactive math options that incorporate the plant theme of this chapter.

TABLE 2.4 Technology Resources for Plants in a Row Activities

RESOURCE	DESCRIPTION	GRADE LEVEL	CODE
PBS Kids: Vegetable Planting	Vegetable Planting game involves counting and comparison of size and quantity with Sid the Science Kid.	K	qrgo.page.link/oMKAe
PBS Kids: Vegetable Harvest	Vegetable Harvest game involves counting and cardinality with Sid the Science Kid.	K	qrgo.page.link/jBNL8
My American Farm	Play games focused about American farming with various math topics embedded throughout. Games for science and other subjects are also available.	K–5	qrgo.page.link/tLHQH

Engineering: Agricultural Engineering

This project offers an opportunity to introduce children to agricultural engineering and to engage them in an engineering challenge of their own. Learning more about the field of agricultural engineering exposes kids to career options that involve many areas of science and applications of mathematics and technology. Kids can learn more about agricultural engineering by reading about different types of engineering and associated resources from TeachEngineering.org or by watching a child-friendly video about agricultural engineering from the National Science Foundation.

Scan the QR codes to learn more about agricultural engineering.

Types of Engineering

Agricultural Engineering
Video from NSF

NGSS Engineering Design Standards

The engineering design challenge in this chapter provides opportunities for children to develop understanding of the NGSS Engineering Design Standards identified here.

K-2 ACTIVITIES	3-5 ACTIVITIES
K-2-ETS1-2. Develop a simple sketch, drawing, or physical model to illustrate how the shape of an object helps it function as needed to solve a given problem.	**3-5-ETS1-1.** Define a simple design problem reflecting a need or a want that includes specified criteria for success and constraints on materials, time, or cost.

To engage in some engineering design of their own, children can design and create a plant watering system for an indoor plant. Keeping in mind that the nature of engineering is to design solutions to problems, the problem that kids are challenged to solve is to automatically water a plant. Common materials can be used to solve this problem, including empty two-liter bottles, water bottles, straws, or tubing and the plants that children grew for the science activities in this project (see Figure 2.9). Teachers and families can look online for ideas that might offer some kid-friendly suggestions, but it is important that children be the ones to use their creativity, knowledge, and skills to complete this challenge. Over-scaffolding or turning the engineering activity into a step-by-step process removes the element of challenge that invites engineering thinking and learning.

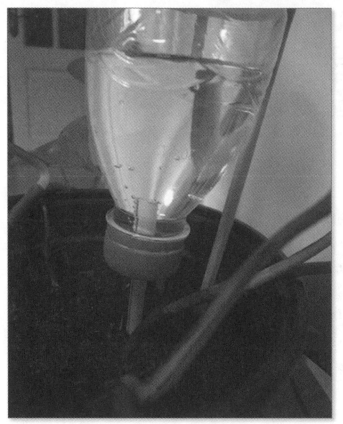

Figure 2.9 An automatic plant waterer could be engineered with a bottle and straw.

Adults should provide loose guidance as children progress through the engineering design process of Ask-Imagine-Plan-Create-Improve (Museum of Science, Boston, 2020). As part of the engineering design process, children must formulate their own questions, brainstorm possible solutions, draw pictures, and consider what plans may or may not work. Then, children choose their best design idea to create their watering system, test it, and discuss how it could be improved. Ask older children to think in advance about how they will know if their solution truly works or not. Some criteria could include gauging the dampness of the soil or monitoring successful plant growth.

Extensions and Connections

Entertainment. Games about gardening and farming have become extremely popular in recent years and include Farming Simulators, Farmville, Gardening Mama, and Animal Crossing. Movies such as *The Lorax*, *The Secret Garden*, and *Peter Rabbit* also extend the plant theme in this project. Science-focused children's programs such as *Bill Nye the Science Guy* and *Sid the Science Kid* can both educate and entertain children. These types of entertainment may not stand alone, but they can add to and potentially extend kids' enjoyment of what they learn in this project.

Children's Literature. Many children's books have been written about plants, flowers, gardens, and farms. Any high-quality children's book focused on those topics can help extend the science learning in this book. Some possibilities are *The Dandelion Seed* by Joseph Anthony, Dianna Hutts Aston's *A Seed is Sleepy*, *Tree of Life* by Barbara Bash, *The Blue Roses* by Linda Boyden, *The Tiny Seed* by Eric Carle, and *From Seed to Plant* by Gail Gibbons.

Writing. After exploring plant growth, children can summarize what they learned by writing informational text about how a plant grows. In the early grades, writing will be accompanied by drawings, while older children should support their story with facts and definitions obtained through their online research and exploration.

Fine Arts. For young children, rhyming songs such as *Old MacDonald Had a Farm* and *The Farmer in the Dell* can be thematic sing-along accompaniments to this project. Children of all ages can create artwork with plants as the focus. Drawings, collages, and paintings of flowers and plants can be adapted for learners of all ages to incorporate visual arts in the project.

Computer Science. Children can use block programming such as MIT's Scratch to create their own simple games or simulations where they water a plant or give it sunshine on screen. In a more real-world setting, children with access to a BBC micro:bit can create a temperature or moisture probe for their plant, perhaps in combination with the automatic plant watering engineering design challenge.

What's Cooking?

According to a popular saying, "Baking is science; cooking is art." While it's true that baking requires a level of precision characteristic of science, both baking and cooking involve science (and many opportunities for STEM learning) and both can be quite artistic as well. Cooking and baking involve mixtures, solutions, chemical reactions, measurement, fractions, money, counting, iterative design, and a range of technologies that make it all possible. In this project, children will explore STEM by making a recipe of their own. Amidst heightened food insecurity such as many have experienced during the COVID-19 pandemic, teachers should be especially mindful of cooking and food suggestions. The hands-on experience of cooking is valuable but should not inflict further distress on children and families.

ISTE Standards for Students

The uses of technology in this chapter are most aligned with the following ISTE Standards for Students. Some of the technology learning opportunities in this chapter are specific to science and math content. Students can also use many technologies to present and share their learning. Tools such as discussion boards and student-generated multimedia presentations (e.g., podcasts, videos) could be used to support technology learning regardless of specific math or science content.

Empowered Learner

1c. Students use technology to seek feedback that informs and improves their practice and to demonstrate their learning in a variety of ways.

Knowledge Constructor

3d. Students build knowledge by actively exploring real-world issues and problems, developing ideas and theories and pursuing answers and solutions.

Innovative Designer

4d. Students exhibit a tolerance for ambiguity, perseverance and the capacity to work with open-ended problems.

Materials, Time, and Supervision

Cooking can be a rich cultural and educational experience. This chapter offers recipe suggestions, but the actual ingredients and supplies for cooking can and should be reflective of children, their families, and their cultures. Since this chapter focuses on processes that are not specific to any one recipe, teachers can offer the provided recipe suggestions, but encourage families to substitute the recipes for what is available and culturally relevant to their children. Families can include children in preparing virtually any recipes that involve mixing, heating, and cooling ingredients. Depending on the amount of time invested each day, activities in this chapter could be accomplished in a week or slightly more. Recipe choices will also dictate the level of adult supervision that is appropriate. Of course, it's important to exercise caution to ensure that children are safe when kitchen tools such as knives or stoves are required. Families' dietary choices may be another concern in this unit, but activities are easily adaptable for a variety of dietary and cultural traditions.

The recipes in this chapter require the following items but could easily be substituted for other family recipes (Table 3.1).

TABLE 3.1 Project Materials

REQUIRED MATERIALS
• Connected device (laptop, desktop, tablet, or smartphone)
• 1 gallon-size freezer bag
• 1 quart-size freezer bag
Note: See individual recipes for specific ingredients.

Resources to Explore and Inspire

Modern kitchens are full of technology, from basic heating and cooling devices to innovative Wi-Fi-enabled smart appliances. Children may use some of these kitchen technologies, but educationally-focused technology explorations are used to launch and support this project. Table 3.2 summarizes online resources teachers and families might use to introduce the context of the activity, extend learning, and incorporate after science explorations to expand on scientific ideas.

TABLE 3.2 Resources to Explore: What's Cooking?

RESOURCE	DESCRIPTION	GRADE LEVEL	CODE
TED-Ed	*Chemistry of Cookies* video explains some of the science of cooking in child-friendly language.	K–5	qrgo.page.link/Xfs4A
Kids Cooking Activities	Online collection of cooking activities, recipes, lessons, and ideas for children of all ages, with specific supports for pre-readers.	K–5	qrgo.page.link/F35MC

(Continued)

RESOURCE	DESCRIPTION	GRADE LEVEL	CODE
Exploratorium Science Museum	Science of Cooking collection of online cooking activities.	3–5	qrgo.page.link/zkUm8
Smithsonian Science Education Center	Pick Your Plate! A Global Guide to Nutrition interactive game offers a broader social context for food and learning in this chapter.	4–5	qrgo.page.link/B67pc

Science: Heating, Cooling, and Mixing

Science learning about cooking could connect with a variety of standards. This chapter focuses on properties of materials, changes caused by heating and cooling, and mixtures.

Getting Started

Lead science learning for this activity by engaging children in hands-on cooking. Figure 3.1 offers a flexible recipe for cookies. The recipe suggestions in this project can be adapted for a variety of diets including vegan, nut-free, and gluten-free. Children could also prepare an alternative family recipe or assist adults with daily meal preparation instead. Scientifically, the activities emphasize properties of matter and physical/chemical changes.

NO-BAKE COOKIES

3 cups	rolled oats
1 cup	peanut butter, almond butter, or tahini
1 cup	honey, maple syrup, or agave
1 cup	chocolate chips

Combine nut butter/tahini and honey/syrup in microwave-safe bowl. Microwave 30–45 seconds and stir well. Microwave another 30 seconds if not soft enough to stir easily.

In large bowl, pour oats and add microwaved mixture. Mix well, add ½ cup of chocolate chips and stir until incorporated.

Use a scoop, spoon, or clean hands to make 20 balls of cookie dough, placing each on a cookie sheet or wax paper. Flatten each cookie using a spoon or the bottom of a glass. Sprinkle the rest of the chocolate chips on top of cookies. Refrigerate at least 1 hour.

Figure 3.1 Students and families can adapt and make No-Bake Cookies.

NGSS Disciplinary Core Ideas for Science

Science learning in this chapter aligns with the standards shown here. The standards emphasize actively engaging in science, including verbs such as *plan* and *conduct*, construct an argument, make observations, and conduct an investigation. Thus, it is especially important that children have opportunities to do hands-on science and discuss their scientific thinking with teachers, peers, or family members.

K-2 ACTIVITIES	3-5 ACTIVITIES
2-PS1-1. Plan and conduct an investigation to describe and classify different kinds of materials by their observable properties.	**5-PS1-3.** Make observations and measurements to identify materials based on their properties.
2-PS1-4. Construct an argument with evidence that some changes caused by heating or cooling can be reversed and some cannot.	**5-PS1-4.** Conduct an investigation to determine whether the mixing of two or more substances results in new substances.

Grade-Level Guidelines

Over the course of a week or two, children can participate in a number of cooking experiences that give them a chance to discuss and learn science. Some of these are formal activities explained in this chapter, but informal activities such as helping plan and prepare meals are also beneficial. As with many science activities, emphasis should be placed on doing, exploring, discussing, and reflecting.

Grades K–2

To draw young learners' attention to properties of matter, ask questions about the color, texture, hardness, and flexibility of foods and ingredients in their recipes. Have them record their observations in a science journal or in a shareable document (handwritten, written online, or recorded as an audio/video journal to reflect and share). Also ask children to make predictions about properties of their mixtures and finished recipes:

- What do they think will happen when two ingredients are mixed together?

- Can the mixture be undone?

- What happens to an ingredient you can't see anymore?

Exploring some of the online resources in Table 3.3 can help adults identify questions to ask and topics to discuss with children.

Another opportunity for science learning involves the changes caused by heating and cooling. With the No-Bake Cookies (Figure 3.2), ask children about the changes that occur when the nut butter/syrup mixture is heated in the microwave or after refrigerating the finished cookies. Ask whether those changes can be reversed. For example, refrigerating and then bringing the cookies back to room temperature is a reversible change. Incorporate the question, *Can this change be reversed?* when preparing other recipes and meals. Water and butter can change from liquid to solid and back again with temperature changes. However, a cooked egg can't be uncooked. And a cooked carrot will never return to the crunchiness of a raw carrot. While young children need not yet fully understand the chemical processes that result in reversible and irreversible changes, observing and constructing arguments about changes lays the foundation for deeper understanding of chemical reactions in later grades.

TABLE 3.3 Science Resources for Heating, Cooling, and Mixing Activities

RESOURCE	DESCRIPTION	GRADE LEVEL	CODE
Young Chef's Kitchen	Lesson plans, videos, recipes, and, kitchen science experiments.	K–5	qrgo.page.link/RVJWn
Michigan State University Extension	Ideas and guidelines highlighting the science of candy making.	K–5	qrgo.page.link/Rdfr7
Scientific American	Short video explanation of the chemistry of the Maillard reaction and how it changes flavors.	3–5	qrgo.page.link/asZUi

Figure 3.2 Children can mix and make their own no-bake cookies.

Grades 3–5

Cooking is an ideal context to investigate mixtures, solutions, and chemical versus physical changes. For example, adding chocolate chips to the No-Bake Cookies results in a mixture with physical changes. But baking chocolate chip cookies results in chemical changes as the heat from the oven interacts with the eggs, flour, and chocolate chips during baking. To extend this over time, ask children to help prepare a meal and discuss whether mixing ingredients results in a new substance. Simple vegetable and fruit salads are good examples of physical changes using foods that children can easily help prepare. Children can also prepare a bag of microwave popcorn and note the chemical changes that occur as the kernels pop. Table 3.3 offers additional resources that will help teachers, families, and children further unpack scientific concepts within cooking.

Math: Combining with Whole Numbers and Fractions

Cooking is as rich a context for learning math as it is for science. Let's take the No-Bake Cookie recipe as an example. Children must measure ingredients in 1-cup increments, count 3 cups if they are using a 1-cup measure, divide chocolate chips in half, measure and interpret time for the microwave and in the refrigerator, count the number of cookies (and likely arrange them in rows on a cookie sheet), and divide the remaining ½ cup of chocolate chips relatively evenly among 20 cookies. But most children won't notice or think deeply about the math involved in that recipe if they are not prompted to do so.

Getting Started

The mathematical connections highlighted here can be adapted for any recipe. But what's important is to help children mathematize and unpack the mathematics in what they are doing. Doing so will help children connect between math in real life and math in school. If this project accompanied a fraction unit in math class, many children could successfully determine that it takes 6 measures of ¼ cup each to make 1½ cups but struggle with the problem $6 \times ¼ =$ ___. Although many math textbooks and worksheets start with symbolic problems (e.g., $6 \times ¼ =$ ___) and work up to word problems, introducing concepts with contexts can better support students' understanding. Children can picture and experiment with actual cups and measures, allowing them to make sense of fractions and fraction multiplication. Purposeful scaffolding and connections are important for helping kids realize how their fraction experiences when cooking relate to the fractions they see in their textbook or worksheet. Teachers and parents can help identify and emphasize those connections to support mathematical learning.

CCSSM Math Content Standards

Many mathematics connections are possible within the cooking context. During cooking activities, connect to mathematical ideas about counting, measurement, time, and fractions. Math activities in this project support math standards in K–5, as shown here.

K–2 ACTIVITIES	3–5 ACTIVITIES
CCSS.MATH.CONTENT.K.CC.B.4. Understand the relationship between numbers and quantities; connect counting to cardinality.	**CCSS.MATH.CONTENT.3.MD.A.1.** Tell and write time to the nearest minute and measure time intervals in minutes. Solve word problems involving addition and subtraction of time intervals in minutes, e.g., by representing the problem on a number line diagram.
CCSS.MATH.CONTENT.K.CC.B.4.A. When counting objects, say the number names in the standard order, pairing each object with one and only one number name and each number name with one and only one object.	**CCSS.MATH.CONTENT.3.NF.A.3.** Explain equivalence of fractions in special cases, and compare fractions by reasoning about their size.
CCSS.MATH.CONTENT.1.MD.B.3. Tell and write time in hours and half-hours using analog and digital clocks.	**CCSS.MATH.CONTENT.3.NF.A.3.A.** Understand two fractions as equivalent (equal) if they are the same size, or the same point on a number line.
CCSS.MATH.CONTENT.2.MD.C.7. Tell and write time from analog and digital clocks to the nearest five minutes, using a.m. and p.m.	**CCSS.MATH.CONTENT.4.NF.B.3.** Understand a fraction a/b with a > 1 as a sum of fractions 1/b.
CCSS.MATH.CONTENT.2.G.A.3. Partition circles and rectangles into two, three, or four equal shares, describe the shares using the words halves, thirds, half of, a third of, etc., and describe the whole as two halves, three thirds, four fourths. Recognize that equal shares of identical wholes need not have the same shape.	**CCSS.MATH.CONTENT.4.NF.B.4.** Apply and extend previous understandings of multiplication to multiply a fraction by a whole number.
	CCSS.MATH.CONTENT.5.NF.B.7.C. Solve real world problems involving division of unit fractions by non-zero whole numbers and division of whole numbers by unit fractions, e.g., by using visual fraction models and equations to represent the problem.

Grade-Level Guidelines

Not every recipe or cooking experience invites connections to all of the math standards that are identified, but most can be easily adapted to do so. Let's use the No-Bake Cookies recipe as an example of how to address standards for different grades during cooking experiences.

Grades K–2

Two foundational number concepts for young learners are *cardinality* and *one-to-one correspondence,* and counting cookies or any other foods can help young children learn these important counting concepts (Figure 3.3). A child who does not yet have a grasp of cardinality could be asked to count 20 cookies and success-fully count them one by one. Yet when asked afterward how many cookies there are, they would begin counting all over again, not realizing that the last number (20) answered the "how many" question. Similarly, one-to-one correspondence associates one number with each item in a set, rather than rote counting in ways that may not correspond with the items being counted. You can help children develop these skills by having them measure ingredients by whole numbers and count out the cookies they make. When children measure 3 cups of oats for the No-Bake Cookies using a 1-cup measure, ask them to count each cup as they add it to the bowl and, after all oats are added, ask, *"How many cups of oats did you put in the bowl?"*

Figure 3.3 Children can learn cardinality and one-to-one correspondence when counting food.

Virtually any activity can be mathematized to emphasize time, and cooking is no different. The level of precision will differ according to children's ages, so adults may need to "stack the deck" a bit for younger learners. Try to time it so that the No-Bake Cookies go into the refrigerator on the hour or half-hour and ask the child what time it is. Then ask again what time it is when the cookies have set (at least an hour later).

Measuring ingredients is a rich context for children to learn about fractions. Of course, measurement concepts are another obvious connection to be made, but this project emphasizes counting, time, and fractions instead. The No-Bake Cookies recipe calls for whole cups, making it more accessible to very young learners. Chocolate chips are split in half (half in the mixture, half on top of the finished cookies), offering an early fraction introduction.

Grades 3–5

Older learners will learn to tell time to the nearest five-minute or minute level of precision. You can also create elapsed time problems while cooking. For example, *"If it's 3:25 now and the cookies need to refrigerate for an hour, what time will the cookies be done?"* Of course, most recipe time intervals are not full hours, so different time intervals increase the complexity of the question. Notice the difference between the previous example and *"If it's 3:27 now and the cookies need to bake for 14 minutes, what time will the cookies be done?"* Be mindful of details such as these when determining whether a math opportunity is developmentally appropriate or sufficiently challenging for the child.

To draw out more fraction work, limit the measuring cups or ask children to scale the recipe. The finished No-Bake Cookie recipe makes 20 cookies, so ask a third grader to adapt the recipe to make only 10 cookies. This will require half cups and, for the chocolate chips, half of a half cup. You can emphasize equivalent fractions and conceptualizing a fraction a/b as a copies of size $1/b$ by only having a ¼ cup measure available. In this case, the halved recipe will call for 1 ½ cups of oats. Children will need to consider how many ¼ cups comprise 1 ½ cups and may think of it as 6/4. This means that each measure is ¼ and it will take 6 measures of size ¼ to make 6/4 or 1 ½ cups (Figure 3.4).

You can also connect to fraction multiplication by using careful language such as, *"You had to fill the ¼ cup measuring cup with oats six times to measure 6/4 or 1 ½ cups,"* and ask children how that helps them make sense of $6 \times ¼ = 1 ½$ or 6/4. Another opportunity to think about fractions and operations when cooking relates to portioning. Division and fractions can easily relate to sharing, and many textbook word problems reference cookies. With the No-Bake Cookie recipe, ask children how many cookies each person would get if they have to share among 4 friends, 5 friends, or even 6 friends. Or, when forming the cookies into balls, divide the dough in half and save half for later.

Figure 3.4 Measuring ingredients can help children understand fractions.

Engineering: Chemical Engineering

Types of Engineering for Kids' Exploration

This project is a perfect opportunity for kids to learn about the career field of chemical engineering. Chemical engineers work in a variety of contexts, including environmental, pharmaceutical, energy, and food! Scan the QR code to learn more about what chemical engineers do.

How People Make
Macaroni

Food-related engineering also includes manufacturing, which
children can explore by watching publicly available factory visit
videos. Scan the QR code to watch a video about making macaroni from *Mr. Rogers' Neighborhood.*

NGSS Engineering Design Standards

The engineering design challenge in this chapter provides opportunities for children to
develop understanding of the NGSS Engineering Design Standards identified here.

K–2 ACTIVITIES	3–5 ACTIVITIES
K-2-ETS1-3. Analyze data from tests of two objects designed to solve the same problem to compare the strengths and weaknesses of how each performs.	**3-5-ETS1-2.** Generate and compare multiple possible solutions to a problem based on how well each is likely to meet the criteria and constraints of the problem.

Ice cream taste testers (what some might call the best job ever) typically earn
college degrees in chemistry or food sciences before helping ice cream makers
create the tastiest products. Testing properties (much like children did in the science
activities for this project) and making iterative improvements to recipes helps create
ice cream that looks, smells, and tastes delicious. Children can do the same as they
make and test their own homemade ice cream. Families may have or find their
own homemade ice cream recipes that involve an ice cream machine, bags, or cans.
Figure 3.5 is a homemade ice cream recipe that children could make using simple
ingredients and two plastic bags. Families who do not eat dairy could replace the
half-and-half with an alternative milk (soy, almond, coconut, or cashew milk),
though the texture of the resulting ice cream is likely to differ.

HOMEMADE ICE CREAM IN A BAG

Materials

1 gallon-size freezer bag

1 quart-size freezer bag

Ice (2–3 cups)

½ cup salt (rock salt is best, but regular salt also works)

Ingredients

1 cup cream or half-and-half

2 tablespoons sugar

½ teaspoon vanilla flavoring

2 tablespoons flavoring (chocolate chips, raspberry syrup, fruit, etc.)

Combine all ingredients in the quart-size bag and seal. Fill the gallon-size bag half-full of ice and sprinkle the salt over the ice. Put the quart-sized bag full of ingredients inside the larger bag with the ice and salt. Make sure both are well sealed (you can double-bag the ingredients or seal with duct tape to be extra sure). Shake the bag (about 7–10 minutes) until the ingredients turn into soft ice cream.

Taste and test for properties such as color, flavor, texture, and smell. How could you make the ice cream even better next time?

Figure 3.5 Making homemade ice cream in a bag can be a food engineering learning opportunity.

To emphasize the engineering design process during this activity, ask children to make and compare two variations or iterations of the recipe and compare strengths and weaknesses of each. Adults and children can work together throughout this food engineering process (see Figure 3.6). Older children could also create a rubric for evaluating their ice cream according to specific criteria (e.g., sweetness, creaminess, color, or how quickly it melts). Doing so will help to identify criteria for success in advance and more closely relate with the engineering design process and the elementary Engineering Design Standards. Other options for engaging in engineering within the food context include creating a device that defrosts an ice cube faster, creating a solar cooker or a Rube Goldberg machine that flips a cookie, or taking apart an old kitchen device (with adult help and safety first!) to see what engineers had to put together to make something like a salad spinner or toaster.

Figure 3.6 Elementary children can work with adults to design and test their own ice cream recipes.

Extensions and Connections

Entertainment. To help set the stage for the cooking project, families can select movies or television programs that they feel are appropriate and interesting for their children. Examples of G- or PG-rated movies that focus on cooking include: *Ratatouille* (G), *No Reservations* (PG), *Mostly Martha* (PG), *The Hundred-Foot Journey* (PG), and *Cloudy with a Chance of Meatballs* (PG). Many television programs on various networks now focus on children and cooking, such as *Chopped Junior, MasterChef Junior, Kids Baking Championship, Top Chef Junior, Food Network Star Kids, Rachael Ray's Kids' Cook-Off, Kids BBQ Championship,* and *Be Our Chef.* Another option to leverage entertainment that is related to the theme of this project is through video games. Some game possibilities include: *Cooking Mama* and *Food Network: Cook or Be Cooked* for Nintendo systems; *Overcooked* for Microsoft Windows, PlayStation, Xbox, or Nintendo; or *Cooking Simulator* for play on most computers.

Children's Literature. Children's books about food and cooking can be paired with this STEM project. Some examples include *Cloudy with a Chance of Meatballs* by Judi Barrett, *Yasmin the Chef* by Saadia Faruqi, *Pancakes, Pancakes!* by Eric Carle, *Thunder Cake* by Patricia Polacco, *Dragons Love Tacos* by Adam Rubin, *Bee-bim Bop!* by Linda Sue Park, *Strega Nona* by Tomie dePaola, *Bilal Cooks Daal* by Aisha Saeed, and *Fry Bread: A Native American Family Story* by Kevin Noble Maillard. Many other possibilities exist and could be used to extend the theme or incorporate STEM-based questions that support the content within this project. A nonfiction option that specifically aligns with this project is *Cooking & Science for Elementary Students* by Kathleen and Kelly Julicher.

Writing. Children may be accustomed to writing stories and narrative text, and those types of writing could be focused on various topics involving food or cooking. This project also invites alternatives that could engage children in writing but in a format with perhaps more novelty: asking children to design and write their own menu either for a fictitious restaurant or even for your family meals. Students could also compile recipes into a family cookbook. This sort of informative writing would emphasize processes and chronological order for making their family's favorite foods and might well serve as a treasured keepsake or homemade gift.

Social Studies. Food and cooking are important aspects of culture. Students can investigate culinary traditions from countries around the world, learning more about people and cultures through the foods people eat and how they are prepared. This could include exploring children's own family and cultural traditions or helping prepare dishes from countries or regions where their ancestors live or lived.

Fine Arts. Children can visit carlwarner.com/photographer/?foodscape-commissions and view artwork from Carl Warner, specifically the Foodscape Commissions and Pizzascape pages. Adults or children can select one or more pieces of art, and children can consider what foods they see in the artwork. To translate into creating their own artwork, challenge the child to create a piece of artwork in the style of Carl Warner using photographs, magazine clippings, drawings—or food!

Oh My Stars!

For thousands of years, the night sky has been a source of wonder and intrigue, and the desire to understand it has led to major advancements in science, technology, engineering, and mathematics. This project will spark and extend children's curiosity about space. The chapter suggests technologies to support exploration of the night sky; science investigations to understand patterns and relationships among the sun, moon, stars, and planets; mathematics tasks focused on the base-ten number system and operations; and an engineering design challenge to build their own telescope or planetarium.

· ·

ISTE Standards for Students

The uses of technology in this chapter are most aligned with the following ISTE Standards for Students. Science activities recommend that children use technology to create and share their own weather forecast. Technology learning is also supported when students maintain journals online, engage in synchronous or asynchronous discussion with peers using various tools, or choose digital artifacts to extend and communicate their knowledge.

Empowered Learner

1c. Students use technology to seek feedback that informs and improves their practice and to demonstrate their learning in a variety of ways.

Knowledge Constructor

3a. Students plan and employ effective research strategies to locate information and other resources for their intellectual or creative pursuits.

3d. Students build knowledge by actively exploring real-world issues and problems, developing ideas and theories and pursuing answers and solutions.

Computational Thinker

5b. Students collect data or identify relevant data sets, use digital tools to analyze them, and represent data in various ways to facilitate problem-solving and decision-making.

Innovative Designer

4d. Students exhibit a tolerance for ambiguity, perseverance and the capacity to work with open-ended problems

· ·

Materials, Time, and Supervision

Table 4.1 lists the materials required to engage with this activity, as well as those for projects that children can elect to do, depending on time constraints, interest, and availability of materials. As always, adults should be mindful of safety considerations as students engage with sharp objects or materials that might break, such as lenses. Students who live in locations with obstructed skies or major light pollution may benefit from a night visit to a location where they can more easily view the night sky, but digital alternatives are also provided if this is not accessible.

TABLE 4.1 Project Materials

REQUIRED	OPTIONAL
• Connected device (laptop, desktop, tablet, or smartphone) • Writing utensil (pen, pencil) • Paper • Crayons, colored pencils, or markers	• Styrofoam ball • Long tube (empty paper towel or gift wrap cardboard tube) • Duct tape • Two convex or magnifying glass lenses (preferably different sizes) • Black or dark umbrella • Object to poke holes through fabric (needle, sharp pencil, etc.) • Smartphone or tablet • Telescope

The project is designed for a few hours each day over one or two weeks, plus some night observations when possible. Ideally, the project would span over the course of at least two weeks so that children can collect observational data over a longer span of time. Children can complete most of the activities with some adult support to get started and then work independently. Night sky viewings and the engineering project may require additional adult supervision to ensure safety, especially for young children.

Resources to Explore and Inspire

Technology and space seem synonymous in many ways. From innovative ideas for space travel to increasingly precise ways of viewing planets and stars, technology continues to expand the human understanding of space. We can also use technology to expand children's understanding of space and to pique their interest in learning more. Children can visit the NASA website or YouTube channel or watch NASA TV to find an amazing amount of information about outer space, such as videos of spacewalks, educational talks from astronauts aboard the International Space Station, and information about aspects of daily life in space such as eating, sleeping, or toilets.

The science activities in this chapter reference additional technologies that can help children observe the night sky. Online applications or mobile apps for smartphones or tablets allow children to identify stars and planets, and many of these apps include augmented reality to identify constellations and other objects in the sky.

Examples of such apps include Star Gazer+, Star Walk, and Sky Guide. These sorts of technologies can augment children's observations of the night sky or allow them to see what might not otherwise be visible from some locations. Table 4.2 summarizes some of the technology resources that educators and families may find useful throughout this chapter.

TABLE 4.2 Resources to Explore: Oh My Stars!

RESOURCE	DESCRIPTION	GRADE LEVEL	CODE
NASA for Educators	Collection of space-focused online resources, games, and activities.	K–5	qrgo.page.link/6pnuQ
Jet Propulsion Lab (JPL)	Space-focused STEM education resources, such as classroom and family activities, demonstrations, games, and labs.	K–5	qrgo.page.link/PELZg
Stellarium	View live, on-screen representations of the night sky from any location.	K–5	qrgo.page.link/oA5aq
NASA STEAM Innovation Lab	Connects educators, families, and children with digital learning using cutting-edge technologies.	3–5	qrgo.page.link/RTMyx

Science: Sun, Moon, and Stars

Science activities in this project emphasize observation, predictable patterns, and the relationship of the sun's brightness and distance from Earth. Certainly it's possible to discover many more scientific concepts through space-themed activities, and children may make additional scientific observations during this project. To help them keep track of their discoveries and progress, have students keep a night sky observation journal throughout the project; what they include in the journal will depend on the grade level.

NGSS Disciplinary Core Ideas for Science

Encourage K–2 children to observe predictable patterns involving the sun, moon, and stars. In later elementary grades, children should make observations about the brightness of stars to help support an argument about the sun, other stars, and relative distance from Earth.

K-2 ACTIVITIES	3-5 ACTIVITIES
1-ESS1-1. Use observations of the sun, moon, and stars to describe patterns that can be predicted.	**5-ESS1-1.** Support an argument that differences in the apparent brightness of the sun compared to other stars is due to their relative distances from Earth.

Getting Started

Throughout the science exploration for this project, be sure to emphasize prediction, observation, patterns children notice, and discussions about those patterns. This project can be paired with more traditional bookwork about moon phases, planets, and stars. The observations and inquiry in this project may well help children make better sense of the space science in their school curriculum—after all, capturing observations of the stars and moon can be quite difficult during normal school hours. The science learning in this activity can also be extended into the real world of citizen science, a way to crowdsource scientific discovery by inviting public participation in solving real-world problems.

Grade-Level Guidelines

Children of all ages can observe patterns in moon phases, sunrise and sunset, and relative location of planets and stars in the night sky. A telescope can be a useful tool for assisting with children's observations. Using an online virtual planetarium or stargazing app can help identify specific stars, planets, and constellations that might be otherwise difficult for children to distinguish in the night sky. Of course, things like sunset, sunrise, and moon phases are more easily observable if one has a clear view of the sky and agreeable weather.

Grades K–2

Beginning at young ages, children can observe and track the moon each night. If the moon is not visible (because of factors such as weather, location, visual disability, or bedtime), digital stargazing or planetarium tools, weather forecasting apps, and online sites can provide the needed information in a variety of formats. After one week of observing the moon, children should be able to observe differences, and two full weeks of observations offer even more noticeable changes. Because the focus in grades K–2 is on describing predictable patterns, be sure to ask questions that highlight patterns:

- What do you notice?

- What do you predict will happen next time?

- How does your prediction compare to what you observed?

- Is there a pattern in your observations? How do you know?

Encourage children to justify their predictions with observational evidence and discuss patterns they notice.

Young children may wonder if the moon actually changes shape each night. What a fun discussion can be had on this topic! To further explore why the appearance of the moon changes each night, try having children act out the phases of the moon in an activity from the Jet Propulsion Lab (QR code in Table 4.4) using only a pencil, a white Styrofoam ball, a light, and a dark room. Activities such as these also provide an opportunity to introduce formal science vocabulary such as *waxing, waning, crescent, gibbous, new moon,* and *full moon.*

Alternatively, observations could focus on sunrise and sunset. It's unlikely for most times and locations that elementary children will be awake to observe both the sunrise and sunset, so instead, have children observe and collect data about the sunrise or the sunset, or look up data from online sources or weather forecasts on television.

Grades 3–5

Children in older grades can make observations about the relative brightness of stars as compared to the sun. Observing the night sky might begin with noticing when the first "star" appears in the sky. However, virtual planetariums and star-gazing apps will reveal that the first visible "star" isn't usually a star at all, but rather a planet. As the sky darkens, students may take note of stars that shine brightest and those that are barely visible. Ask children to consider why they think some stars appear brighter than others. Some likely responses will include the size of stars (e.g., bigger stars look brighter), the distance of stars from Earth (e.g., closer stars look brighter), or just that some stars are brighter than others (just as some lights are brighter than others). The eventual goal is for children to make an argument, using evidence, that observable brightness of stars depends on the relative distance from Earth. Rather than telling children this, let them discover and make this argument themselves based on authentic data they gather with the assistance of technology. Frequently ask questions to help children make these realizations:

- What do you notice?

- What do you wonder?

- Is there a pattern?

- What does the data show?

The vastness of the night sky, as well as measurement/location precision accessible to most elementary children, can make documenting these observations quite challenging. With adult permission and supervision, children might use tools embedded within sites or apps. Adult guidance is especially important for sites that are not designed for children. Help children safely explore sites that may have unpredictable advertisements embedded, and guide children to find relevant information within advanced sites that may overwhelm young children. For instance, Stellarium has an Observe feature that allows logged in users to maintain an astronomical log book. Depending on the specific digital tool, children may be able to click on specific stars to access the name of the star, its magnitude, distance from Earth, and much additional data. For this activity, it is important that children can identify or look up the names of particular stars, either from constellations (e.g., Big Dipper or Orion's Belt) or through a digital tool.

Prompt children to record the names of the four brightest stars they see and the names of four less bright stars they see. Then ask them to record the distance from Earth for each star they identify. A table, such as the example shown in Table 4.3, can be helpful for recording observations and noticing patterns. Depending on the data points selected, most children should notice that brighter stars are closer to Earth while dimmer stars are farther away. However, beware that these rough observations can be imprecise and some stars that children perceive as bright might actually be more distant than ones that appear less bright. For example, Deneb might look bright in the sky even though it is estimated at 1411.95 light years from Earth! In this particular case, Deneb is a supergiant that is especially luminous. Consider asking the child to collect more data points (list additional stars) to more clearly reveal the relationship between relative distance and apparent brightness.

TABLE 4.3 Sample Star Observation Table

STARS THAT LOOK BRIGHT		STARS THAT DO NOT LOOK BRIGHT	
Name of Star	Distance	Name of Star	Distance
Vega	25.04 light years	Kochab	130.93 light years
Capella	42.80 light years	Sadr	1832.37 light years
Arcturus	36.72 light years	Polaris	432.57 light years
Merak	96.5 light years	Tania Australis	331.27 light years

Source: Stellarium-web.org

After comparing the perceived brightness and relative distance of stars in the night sky, ask children to describe the brightness of the sun (emphasize that they should never look directly at it!) and make predictions about the sun's distance from Earth. Most children will accurately predict that the sun appears brighter, is closer to Earth than the other stars, and is bigger in the sky. However, kids may be surprised to learn just how much closer the sun is—8.3 light *minutes*, or 0.0000158 light years from Earth. Further discussion and exploration might focus on the observable size of the sun from Earth and the fact that our sun lights up the entire sky for several hours each day, whereas even the closest other stars are just a dot in the night sky. If the notion of light years is not familiar to children, they can learn more about it online, at sites such as NASA's Space Place. Table 4.4 summarizes a variety of technology resources that can support the science concepts in this chapter.

TABLE 4.4 Science Resources for Sun, Moon, and Stars Activities

RESOURCE	DESCRIPTION	GRADE LEVEL	CODE
PBS Kids	Space-focused citizen science activities.	K–5	qrgo.page.link/a2rpH
Moon Phases	Online tool with up-to-date information about moon phases.	K–5	qrgo.page.link/VzduA
Jet Propulsion Laboratory	Hands-on moon phases activity.	1–5	qrgo.page.link/mG8Kd
Sky and Telescope	Description of Deneb, a bright but distant star.	3–5	qrgo.page.link/AuaCf
NASA Space Place	Description of what a light year is.	3–5	qrgo.page.link/a48c2

Math: Place Value and Comparison

Understanding space involves understanding a lot of mathematics. Yet, much of that mathematics is far too advanced to be appropriate for elementary children. For instance, the distance between the sun and Earth is 0.0000158, or 1.58×10^{-5} light years. Using this context as an opportunity to talk about scientific notation seems logical and might be accessible to some elementary students. But scientific notation involves understanding decimals, exponents, and negative exponents, and it does not appear in the CCSSM until Grade 8. Instead of focusing on mathematics that is more advanced than many elementary children are ready for, observed data and mathematics history allow us to make more developmentally appropriate mathematics connections.

Getting Started

Adults and children, alike, might be surprised to learn that thousands of years ago, the ancient Babylonian civilization in Mesopotamia had a number system sophisticated enough to compute lunar eclipse occurrences and planetary speeds. Figure 4.1 shows a tablet inscribed with eclipse calculations, dating back more than 2,200 years.

Figure 4.1 This Cuneiform tablet shows eclipse calculations from ancient Babylonians.

CCSSM Math Content Standards

The mathematics in this project emphasizes place value concepts, including the importance of zero and how place value can be used to compare numbers. Math activities in this project support math standards in K–5, as shown here.

K-2 ACTIVITIES	3-5 ACTIVITIES
CCSS.MATH.CONTENT.1.NBT.B.2. Understand that the two digits of a two-digit number represent amounts of tens and ones. **CCSS.MATH.CONTENT.1.NBT.B.3.** Compare two two-digit numbers based on meanings of the tens and ones digits, recording the results of comparisons with the symbols >, =, and <. **CCSS.MATH.CONTENT.2.NBT.A.1.** Understand that the three digits of a three-digit number represent amounts of hundreds, tens, and ones; e.g., 706 equals 7 hundreds, 0 tens, and 6 ones. **CCSS.MATH.CONTENT.2.NBT.A.3.** Read and write numbers to 1,000 using base-ten numerals, number names, and expanded form. **CCSS.MATH.CONTENT.2.NBT.A.4.** Compare two three-digit numbers based on meanings of the hundreds, tens, and ones digits, using >, =, and < symbols to record the results of comparisons.	**CCSS.MATH.CONTENT.4.NBT.A.2.** Read and write multi-digit whole numbers using base-ten numerals, number names, and expanded form. Compare two multi-digit numbers based on meanings of the digits in each place, using >, =, and < symbols to record the results of comparisons. **CCSS.MATH.CONTENT.5.NBT.A.3.A.** Read and write decimals to thousandths using base-ten numerals, number names, and expanded form, e.g., $347.392 = 3 \times 100 + 4 \times 10 + 7 \times 1 + 3 \times (1/10) + 9 \times (1/100) + 2 \times (1/1000)$. **CCSS.MATH.CONTENT.5.NBT.A.3.B.** Compare two decimals to thousandths based on meanings of the digits in each place, using >, =, and < symbols to record the results of comparisons.

What might be even more surprising is that Babylonians managed to do this in a base-sixty number system (as opposed to our base-ten system) and with only two number symbols (as opposed to the ten digits that comprise modern numbers). More surprising still is that the Babylonians had no symbol for zero! Imagine making precise calculations about celestial bodies millions of miles away from Earth without a symbol for zero! Halfway across the world, in what is now Central America, the ancient Mayan civilization devised their own highly precise number system. The ancient Mayans devised a base-twenty number system using only three symbols: a line or stick to represent five, a dot or pebble to represent one, and a shell to represent zero. This was the first known widespread use of a symbol for zero.

You might ask, what does this have to do with teaching elementary kids about math? First of all, communicating basic math history to children conveys that the math they learn was created—it's not some mystical force from another realm. This can help address student perceptions "that mathematics is closed, dead, emotionless, all discovered" (Bidwell, 1993, p. 461). Historical context can, instead, humanize mathematics as a subject that is dynamic, open, and interesting. Secondly, highlighting the mathematical contributions from diverse civilizations around the world communicates that mathematics comes from and belongs to children of all backgrounds. Finally, this specific story about zero in ancient number systems sets the stage for place value learning relating to calculations in astronomy.

Grade-Level Guidelines

One might wonder how Babylonians could make sense of numbers without a zero. Evidence suggests that, since numbers were often used for trade and commerce, interpreting numerals without zeros depended on context (Jones, 1957). Without a symbol for zero in our number system, 12 could mean 12, 102, 120, 1002, 1,000,000,020,000. If you were at the market buying a dozen eggs, you'd recognize 12 to mean twelve. Or, if you're referring to the age of a great-grandparent, 102 is the interpretation that makes the most sense. On the other hand, the distance in kilometers between Venus and Mars (about 120,000,000 km) is not contextually obvious.

But what does zero and comparing numbers by place value have to do with the space theme of this project? For one, both the Babylonians and Mayans applied their advanced number systems to make sophisticated astronomical calculations and predictions that resulted in highly accurate calendars. Zero is an important mathematical advancement, but especially so for the enormous and miniscule quantities in astronomy. Secondly, this example demonstrates how to use context and questions to connect math and science content that may not be as obviously related.

Grades K–2

You can help children in younger grades learn about the importance of zero and apply place value in contexts involving space.

Invite children to think about context and quantity in ways that highlight why place value is important in our number system (Figure 4.2). They help make meaning for common types of tasks children might encounter, and they also invite quantitative reasoning and justification. The first three prompts have obvious correct answers (unless Booker Elementary School has an enormous lunch room). The last three prompts are less obvious. There could be 96, 906, 9,006, or more fish in a pond; many different answers could make sense. And while the last two questions technically have correct answers (1,300 and 239,000, respectively), we wouldn't reasonably expect children to determine the quantities based on context alone. The last three questions show why zero is so important in a place value system.

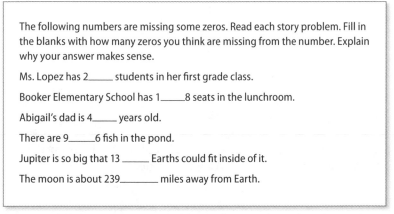

The following numbers are missing some zeros. Read each story problem. Fill in the blanks with how many zeros you think are missing from the number. Explain why your answer makes sense.

Ms. Lopez has 2_____ students in her first grade class.

Booker Elementary School has 1_____8 seats in the lunchroom.

Abigail's dad is 4_____ years old.

There are 9_____6 fish in the pond.

Jupiter is so big that 13 _____ Earths could fit inside of it.

The moon is about 239_____ miles away from Earth.

Figure 4.2 Children solve missing zero problems to deepen understanding of zero and place value.

Children commonly compare numbers using greater than (>), less than (<), or equal (=) symbols, and place value understanding is essential for these comparisons. For example, if comparing two whole numbers with different numbers of digits, the number with more digits is greater. Beware though—this is often generalized to decimals where the rule no longer holds true. Place value understanding also helps kids understand that, when comparing two whole numbers, they should begin by comparing the digits in the greatest place values.

Grades 3–5

Students in later grades can use the data they collect from observing stars to learn and apply operations based on properties of place value. Rather than solving decontextualized "naked number" problems that look like 37 > 25, the same mathematics problem could be contextually posed as: *Write an inequality to show whether Vega or Arcturus is farther away from Earth.* or *Write and solve three questions and inequality problems from the data in the table* (see Table 4.5).

TABLE 4.5 Distances of Selected Stars from Earth

NAME OF STAR	APPROXIMATE DISTANCE FROM EARTH (in Light Years)
Vega	25
Arcturus	37
Capella	43
Merak	100
Kochab	131
Polaris	433
Sadr	1832

Approaching inequalities in this way may be more challenging, but it also provides more opportunity for learning. Students both solve and generate problems, using mathematical notation and comparisons, applying data from tables, and connecting with science content. You can tailor the activity to different grade levels by choosing the data or parameters for collecting data. Whereas the two-digit and three-digit whole numbers in Table 4.5 could be appropriate for first and second graders to compare, the observation data in Table 4.3 includes decimal quantities that are more appropriate for fifth graders to compare.

Engineering: Aerospace Engineering

Types of Engineering for Kids' Exploration

As part of this project, kids can learn about STEM careers related to space. In particular, this is a good chance to learn about the field of aerospace engineering. It's not unusual for kids to dream of being an astronaut when they grow up, but children can scan the QR code to read about the broader range of career possibilities within aerospace engineering and design small-scale projects focused on space.

Elementary children can't engage in the authentic work of aerospace engineers, but they can do fun, classic activities such as making paper airplanes and testing how far they will fly. With the proper materials (two convex lenses or magnifying glasses, a cardboard tube, tape or glue, scissors, and a pencil), kids can engineer their own telescope for observing the night sky. A quick online search of "make a telescope" will yield many variations on this project so that families can appropriately guide children with this challenge. Don't have or can't get two lenses? An alternative space-themed design challenge is to create your own indoor planetarium using a black or dark-colored umbrella, chalk or a pencil, an object sharp enough to pierce the umbrella fabric, a flashlight, and a dark room. To design their own indoor planetarium, children can follow these steps:

1. Use chalk or a pencil to mark the location of prominent stars or constellations on the underside of the opened umbrella.

2. With adult guidance, use a sharp object to poke holes at the locations of the stars. Try to make larger holes for brighter stars and smaller holes for dim stars.

3. Stand under the umbrella in a dark room with a light source above (flashlight or light from a phone or other device).

4. Enjoy your own personal planetarium!

NGSS Engineering Design Standards

The engineering design challenge in this chapter provides opportunities for children to develop understanding of the NGSS Engineering Design Standards identified here.

K-2 ACTIVITIES	3TEACH ENGINEERING5 ACTIVITIES
K-2-ETS1-2. Develop a simple sketch, drawing, or physical model to illustrate how the shape of an object helps it function as needed to solve a given problem	**3-5-ETS1-1.** Define a simple design problem reflecting a need or a want that includes specified criteria for success and constraints on materials, time, or cost.

Extensions and Connections

Entertainment. The list of movies, television programs, and video games about space is far beyond what can be listed here. From blockbuster science fiction franchises to films such as *October Sky* (PG) and Disney Pixar's *WALL-E* (G), many child-friendly space-themed movie options exist. The movie *Hidden Figures* (PG) tells the story about how three African-American women at NASA provided the STEM knowledge for successfully launching astronaut John Glenn into orbit. Television programs such as *Space Racers* or PBS Kids' *Ready Jet Go!* entertain and educate. Many popular video games are also set in space. One that is appropriate for young children and combines science learning with play is *Kerbal Space Program* available for PC, Xbox, and PlayStation platforms.

Children's Literature. To combine reading with this STEM project, children's books about space make good accompaniments. Nonfiction books such as the Who Was? or What Was? series that includes NASA and prominent astronauts and astronomers, child-friendly space encyclopedias and reference books, or books such as *Astrophysics for Young People in a Hurry* by Neil deGrasse Tyson can expand children's understanding related to space and key figures. Margot Lee Shetterly's *Hidden Figures* books for children, *A Moon of My Own* by Jennifer Rustgi, and *Mousetronaut* by astronaut Mark Kelly are other examples of children's books that complement this project.

Writing. Given the wealth of nonfiction children's books about space, children might write about what they learn in a book of their choice, supporting their writing with text-based evidence. Younger children could also make a picture book about their moon phase observations.

Fine Arts. To connect with music, children could listen to space-focused songs from the *Here Comes the Science* album by They Might Be Giants. Challenge children to make up their own song about space. To incorporate visual arts, children could design their own star constellation. Given a dark printout of the night sky and chalk or a white crayon, children could draw a constellation, name it, and make up their own backstory for it.

Computer Science. Block programming such as Scratch or code.org activities can be used to create projects focused on stars, planets, the moon, or space in general. If children have access to codeable robotics such as Sphero or Dash, they could program the bot to orbit around Earth like the moon, or around the sun like a planet. Children with access to an Ozobot could draw a model of planetary orbits and use the bot to rotate while following the marker paths as a planet might.

How's the Weather?

O ne area of science that directly touches our daily lives is weather. We check the weather, choose clothing based on the weather, plan events around the weather, and monitor conditions for safety during extreme weather events. In this project, children will observe, analyze, and describe patterns in weather to learn about climate and atmospheric science. Children will learn and apply math concepts about data as they represent and analyze the weather data they collect. Technology will assist children in exploring and accessing weather information throughout the project. The project culminates in an engineering design project to create a weather station or weather instruments for their own home. Additional content and entertainment connections are provided at the end of this chapter.

....

ISTE Standards for Students

The technology suggestions embedded throughout this project advance students toward the ISTE Standards identified below. Additional ISTE Standards can be addressed through supplemental activities and the use of technology tools for communicating, presenting, and assessing in an online schooling environment.

Empowered Learner

1c. Students use technology to seek feedback that informs and improves their practice and to demonstrate their learning in a variety of ways.

Knowledge Constructor

3c. Students curate information from digital resources using a variety of tools and methods to create collections of artifacts that demonstrate meaningful connections or conclusions.

3d. Students build knowledge by actively exploring real-world issues and problems, developing ideas and theories and pursuing answers and solutions.

Innovative Designer

4c. Students develop, test and refine prototypes as part of a cyclical design process.

4d. Students exhibit a tolerance for ambiguity, perseverance and the capacity to work with open-ended problems

Computational Thinker

5a. Students collect data or identify relevant data sets, use digital tools to analyze them, and represent data in various ways to facilitate problem-solving and decision-making.

....

Materials, Time, and Supervision

To engage with this project, students will need access to materials, listed in Table 5.1. Various options are provided so families can tailor the project to their child and the materials they have available.

TABLE 5.1 Project Materials

REQUIRED	OPTIONAL
• Connected device (laptop, desktop, tablet, or smartphone)	• Camera/smartphone camera
• Writing utensil (pen, pencil)	• Outdoor thermometer
• Paper	• Barometer
• Crayons, colored pencils, or markers	• Water gauge
• Paper cups	
• Craft sticks or straws	
• Tape	
• Scissors	

The entire project can be completed in one week, a few hours each day, but extending activities across two weeks will allow children to collect more days of weather data. Children can complete much of this project independently with an adult nearby to get them started, engage with questions and discussion, and check in on progress. During the engineering design challenge, an adult may be present to ensure safety with tools such as scissors, especially for young learners. Safety should always be considered with observations during inclement weather and weather advisories should be heeded.

Resources to Explore and Inspire

A variety of games and apps can introduce this project. The Kid Weather app would be an appropriate weather app for the activities throughout this project, and it also has trivia and interactive features that kids could explore at the beginning of the project. Table 5.2 includes a few examples of online games, sites, and weather apps geared toward children. Engaging with these sites or games can set the stage for the science, math, and engineering activities that follow in this project.

TABLE 5.2 Resources to Explore: How's the Weather?

RESOURCE	DESCRIPTION	GRADE LEVEL	CODE
PBS Kids: Sid the Science Kid Games	The Weather Surprise is an interactive game for kids to learn about different climates.	K–2	qrgo.page.link/hk57W
Kid Weather App	Real weather app geared for children.	K–5	qrgo.page.link/zRScj
NASA Climate Kids	Games and topics that kids can interact with to learn more about weather and climate.	K–5	qrgo.page.link/2HK82
ABCya Dress for the Weather game	A game where children dress a puppy for different weather conditions.	K–2	qrgo.page.link/EkHdY

Science: Weather Patterns

Maintaining a weather journal is one important portion of the science activities in this chapter, but children should also share their observations, describe patterns, and ask questions. Families might enjoy watching the local weather forecast each day in coordination with making journal observation entries.

Getting Started

To initiate this project and drive interest in the topic, engage in discussions with children around questions and prompts such as:

- What patterns do you notice in your weather journal?

- Tell me about the weather today.

- What do you think the weather will be like tomorrow?

- How do you think the meteorologist on TV knows what the weather is supposed to be like tomorrow?

- Sometimes the weather forecast is wrong. Why do you think it's important to have a forecast even if it might be wrong?

- [Especially if a severe weather event occurs or is predicted] How does knowing the weather forecast for tomorrow help us prepare for tomorrow? OR The weather is supposed to be bad; what do you think we should do to prepare?

NGSS Disciplinary Core Ideas for Science

Science learning in this chapter aligns with the standards shown here. The standards emphasize communicating about science, including verbs such as *describe*, *construct an argument*, and *support an argument*. Thus, it is especially important that children have opportunities to communicate their scientific thinking either in writing or in discussion with teachers, peers, or family members.

K–2 ACTIVITIES	3–5 ACTIVITIES
K-ESS2-1. Use and share observations of local weather conditions to describe patterns over time. **K-ESS3-2.** Ask questions to obtain information about the purpose of weather forecasting to prepare for, and respond to, severe weather.	**3-ESS2.1.** Represent data in tables and graphical displays to describe typical weather conditions expected during a particular season. **3-ESS2.2.** Obtain and combine information to describe climates in different regions of the world.

After observing and discussing weather conditions, patterns, and forecasts, children can utilize technology to share their own weather forecast. Using a smartphone, camera, or online application with video, have the child prepare and deliver their own weather forecast for the following day, based on the patterns they observed in previous days. If making predictions based on patterns is too challenging for a younger child, they can report the observed daily weather instead.

For their weather forecast, encourage children to get creative. For example, have them make a poster for their background, take photos of their weather conditions, and use digital backgrounds. Within videoconferencing software such as Zoom, kids can create their own virtual background by uploading a photo, deliver their forecast in front of the virtual background, and either share it with family and friends via a live videoconference or record the video to share later or submit in an online class. Adapt the task for older children by asking them to include graphical representations in their forecast or to report the weather for two or more locations in the world.

Grade-Level Guidelines

Awareness of the weather and learning the science of weather are related but not quite the same. Notice the action verbs that begin each of the standards in K–5 science standards relating to weather: *use, share, ask questions, represent, obtain and combine,* and *develop.* In order to develop understanding of weather concepts in elementary science standards, children must engage in active learning experiences. Activities in this project provide these sorts of opportunities.

Grades K–2

Science activities for younger learners emphasize weather conditions, patterns, and forecasts. In school, early grades often start the day with routines that include describing the weather, and this can be a regular routine during distance learning as well. To formalize these observations for discussion, ask children to maintain a daily weather journal throughout this unit. This could be part of a science note-book, a standalone worksheet within an online classroom, or a more open-ended opportunity for students to use technology (e.g., Google Docs, Microsoft Word, slide decks) to document their daily observations. Many weather journal templates and graphic organizers can be found online for print or download—just type "weather journal" into your browser and choose from among the many sites and images that result. Early grades' weather journals may include stickers or cut-and-paste images, which may or may not be included in journals for older children.

The weather journal should include days of the week; a way of indicating conditions such as sunniness and cloudiness, windiness, and precipitation; a place to record the daily temperature; and any other observations children might want to include. Ask children to include the location and time of their observations and the season during which the observations take place. If the journal is kept on paper, you might incorporate weather-themed stickers or images that children can cut and paste for each day, as well as a thermometer to color in for the temperature. Figure 5.1 includes examples of the types of images young students could cut and paste into their weather journal, although this is not an exhaustive list of possibilities for weather conditions.

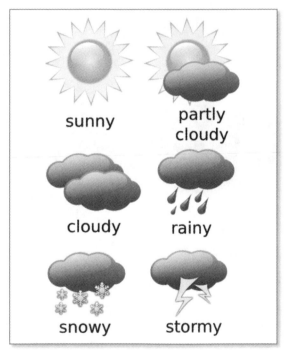

Figure 5.1 Images of weather conditions can be cut and pasted into a weather journal.

The child should complete their weather observation at about the same time each day. This could be first thing in the morning, at lunch, before dinner, or anytime when it is light outside. Because they will be analyzing their data, it is better if there is some consistency in when and where the data is collected. Most often, children can look outside to complete much of their journal (see Figure 5.2). If the family has an outdoor thermometer, they can see the temperature but young children will likely need help learning to read the temperature from a thermometer. Using a thermometer icon that children color in can support learning to read a thermometer, but it may also prove challenging as children represent temperature using a measurement scale rather than simply writing down numerals.

Figure 5.2 Children can observe the weather outside their window each day.

If outdoor observations are not possible or a thermometer is unavailable, use weather apps, preferably ones that are developed to be appropriate for children such as Weather & What to Wear Today, My Weather—For Kids, Kids' Calendar, or Weather Duck. More advanced weather apps are also fine but may provide far more information than children need at this point. Many communities also still have time and temperature phone numbers that will provide temperature data with just a phone call.

Grades 3–5

Children in later elementary grades can also keep a weather journal, but emphasis shifts toward representing data in tables and graphs. To describe climates in different regions around the world, have students include local physical observations, as well as daily data points from distant locations, gathered online or through an app. Older children's weather journals should include tables for organizing the data that they collect. The math activity in this project focuses on interpreting and representing data, so other graphical representations are not necessary in the journal itself.

Table 5.3 illustrates what a weather journal excerpt for older children might include. This example features five locations around the world, in very different climates and regions. Have children choose their own locations, or select diverse locations to help students describe climates in different regions of the world.

TABLE 5.3 Example of a Weather Journal for Children in Grades 3–5

DAILY TEMPERATURE (°F) IN FIVE WORLD LOCATIONS					
Date/Time	Lincoln, Nebraska, USA	Tromsø, Norway	Cusco, Peru	Manila, Philippines	Cairo, Egypt
4/8/2020 9:00am	59	32	59	91	64
4/9/2020 9:30am	45	27	61	86	68
4/10/2020 8:45am	32	27	57	87	61
4/11/2020 10:00am	53	28	64	88	64
4/12/2020 9:00am	34	28	59	86	63

Of course, climate consists of much more than just a week's worth of temperatures, so additional data must be obtained and combined to understand regional climates. To extend conversations about weather to also include climate, students can compare their observations with larger sets of data available through the same online resources students used to collect world weather data (e.g., Weather Underground Historical Weather in Table 5.4). Children can also search online to learn more about climate for their specific locations by simply searching terms such as "Climate + Cusco, Peru." Adults can engage children in discussion about how their data compares with climate data for each location and why there might be discrepancies (e.g., recent weather patterns or climate change).

TABLE 5.4 Science Resources for Weather Patterns Activities

RESOURCE	DESCRIPTION	GRADE LEVEL	CODE
Kids Weather Report	Generate a weather report for your location that uses pictures for emerging readers.	K–2	bit.ly/3pPO98V
Time and Date Weather	Look up current weather conditions for any city.	K–5	bit.ly/393L8fb
Weather Underground Historical Weather	Look up weather conditions for any location and any date since 1930.	K–5	bit.ly/3kVUVGm
National Weather Service	Educational resources for children, including information on satellites, radar, and fire weather.	K–5	bit.ly/335OM4h
Weather Wiz Kids	Child-friendly explanations to questions about weather forecasting.	3–5	bit.ly/3IXLKGQ
Scholastic Teacher Resources	Complete lesson plan about weather forecasting that includes creating first-person weather reports.	3–5	bit.ly/3nLaBOv

Math: Representing and Interpreting Weather Data

Most science experiments and explorations invite the use of measurement and data. These are essential concepts but not heavily emphasized in elementary mathematics curriculum and standards. Instead, math concepts such as numbers, place value, and operations receive the most attention in elementary math. Nevertheless, measurement and data understanding is necessary for scientific and mathematical literacy. Since children collect authentic weather data in the science activity for this chapter, the math activities in this chapter also focus on representing and interpreting data.

CCSSM Math Content Standards

The math activities in this project specifically focus on grade-level mathematics standards about data. Children will use data they collected in their weather observation data.

K-2 ACTIVITIES	3-5 ACTIVITIES
CCSS.MATH.CONTENT.K.MD.B.3. Classify objects into given categories; count the numbers of objects in each category and sort the categories by count.	**CCSS.MATH.CONTENT.3.MD.B.3.** Draw a scaled picture graph and a scaled bar graph to represent a data set with several categories. Solve one- and two-step "how many more" and "how many less" problems using information presented in scaled bar graphs.
CCSS.MATH.CONTENT.1.MD.C.4. Organize, represent, and interpret data with up to three categories; ask and answer questions about the total number of data points, how many in each category, and how many more or less are in one category than in another.	**CCSS.MATH.CONTENT.4.MD.B.4.** Make a line plot to display a data set of measurements in fractions of a unit (1/2, 1/4, 1/8). Solve problems involving addition and subtraction of fractions by using information presented in line plots.
CCSS.MATH.CONTENT.2.MD.D.1. Draw a picture graph and a bar graph (with single-unit scale) to represent a data set with up to four categories. Solve simple put-together, take-apart, and compare problems using information presented in a bar graph.	**CCSS.MATH.CONTENT.5.MD.B.2.** Make a line plot to display a data set of measurements in fractions of a unit (1/2, 1/4, 1/8). Use operations on fractions for this grade to solve problems involving information presented in line plots. For example, given different measurements of liquid in identical beakers, find the amount of liquid each beaker would contain if the total amount in all the beakers were redistributed equally.

Getting Started

Maintaining an organized weather journal as part of the science activities for this chapter provides authentic data for children to work with. Using data students have collected themselves lends more meaning to the mathematics work than hypothetical data that may mean little to the child. Working with small samples of local data children have collected themselves is also consistent with the American Statistical Association's framework for statistics education in elementary grades (Franklin et al., 2005). According to this framework, learning about statistics in elementary grades should focus on components summarized in Table 5.5.

TABLE 5.5 Statistical Learning Process and Recommendations for How's the Weather?

	GENERAL RECOMMENDATIONS	SPECIFIC RECOMMENDATIONS FOR THIS CHAPTER
Formulate Question	Teachers/adults pose questions of interest. Restrict questions to classroom or specific, local context.	Children can participate in formulating questions based on their own weather journal data, but adults should ensure these questions are appropriate statistical questions that invite variation. You might choose things such as comparing high temperatures over time or representing how many days there was precipitation.
Collect Data	Simple experiment. Census of classroom or local context.	Data in children's weather journals are a census of weather conditions in a specific local context over a specified period of time.
Analyze Data	Display variability. Compare individual to individual data points. Compare individual to group data points. Observe association between two variables.	Graph choices should show variability in weather conditions. E.g., Use a pictograph to show the number of days was it sunny, cloudy, or rainy. Students could plot and observe association of two variables such as temperature and time.
Interpret Results	Do not generalize beyond the classroom or local context. Note difference between two individual data points with different conditions. Observe association in displays.	Children should not generalize the weather they observed beyond their own local context. Questions about data representations might include: • Were there more sunny days or rainy days during the last two weeks? • Was today warmer or colder than yesterday?

Table 5.5 highlights a process of understanding data. It may be tempting for adults to jump to familiar statistics and data ideas such as measures of center or sophisticated data representations. However, these may be inaccessible for young children. For instance, calculating a mean requires addition and division, and interpreting or choosing among mean, median, and mode is a deeper concept than computation. Thus, measures of center are not included in math standards until the middle grades. Similarly, scatterplots and line graphs may seem intuitive to adults, but premature for where young children are in their understanding of data. Pie graphs can be especially troublesome and deceptively simple. Young children may be able to interpret existing pie graphs to some extent, but keep in mind that this requires proportional reasoning; and creating a pie graph requires understanding of percentages, angles, and mathematics that many K–5 students may not yet be equipped to apply. Overall, it's important for educators and families to emphasize age-appropriate uses of data rather than rushing to more sophisticated data concepts that may create more confusion than learning.

Grade-Level Guidelines

In elementary grades, math standards combine data and measurement into a single category because the two concepts are related. Important distinctions among data standards across grade levels include the types of data representations students create (picture graphs, bar graphs, line plots), the number of categories in data representations, the level of precision in scale for data representations (nearest whole, half, fourth, etc.), and the types of questions formulated about data. Because the type of data children gather in their weather journals will differ, educators and families may choose to define some statistical questions in advance of the science activity and collect data accordingly. If weather journal data collection is already complete, then adults will need to help children formulate appropriate statistical questions that can be represented and answered from the data students have.

Grades K–2

In early grades, children should classify objects into two to four categories and represent data in picture graphs and bar graphs. (The number of categories increases with grade level.) Children can use the weather conditions data to represent and answer various statistical questions. At this level, children might sort and count how many days were sunny, how many were rainy, and how many were cloudy.

Pictograph Creator

Hand-drawn pictures for pictographs may not all be the same size, but in order for valid visual comparisons, the sizes must be consistent. Have children use grid paper or star stickers to help them create accurate, precise picture graphs. Help them use online tools such as a pictograph creator to generate accurate, precise pictographs from their weather observation data. Scanning the QR code will give you access to Pictograph Creator, a tool that automatically scales the graph and identifies images from basic word searches. However, be aware that some words may not yield the desired images and word variations, so try different wording if you do not find the images that you want (e.g., rain cloud instead of rainy).

Figure 5.3 shows a vertical pictograph with three categories. It is important to vary picture graph orientations so that children can create and interpret data whether arranged horizontally or vertically.

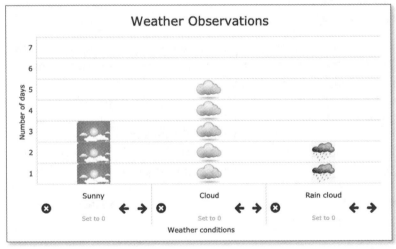

Figure 5.3   Children can create pictographs digitally to represent weather observation data. (Created using primaryschoolict.com/pictograph.)

Be sure to challenge children to answer questions about the graphs they create. For example, the graph in Figure 5.3 invites questions such as:

- How many more cloudy days were there than rainy days?

- How many days were not rainy days?

Grades 3–5

Students will eventually create scaled picture or bar graphs to represent data in several categories. Two weeks of weather observation data may not provide enough data points for a scaled graph to make sense in this activity. To incorporate this type of representation, ask children to look up additional data points, perhaps including an entire month. Data from a longer span of time may also result in more categories as weather conditions will vary more over time in most locations. If children collect local data in a location with little variation in weather conditions, online weather data for an alternative location might also be useful. Weather Underground offers an easy-to-use historical weather search where students could look up weather data by city and date.

By the end of grade 5, children should know how to represent measurement data on dot or line plots and ask questions using that representation. Most online sources list temperature and condition data in decimal values, but line plot data should be represented in fractions, to the nearest ½, ¼, or ⅛ inch to address grade 3–5 math standards. To connect the weather context with math expectations, adults can round data points for a given location to the nearest fraction and provide the data to students in table form, supporting students as they learn about fractions, which are challenging for many children. Students can then represent the given precipitation data using a line plot (Figure 5.4) and pose or answer questions such as:

- What is the total amount of precipitation during the time frame?

- How many days had more than 1¼ inch of precipitation?

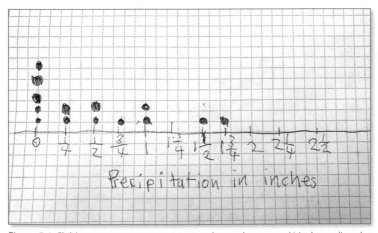

Figure 5.4 Children can represent precipitation data to the nearest ¼ inch on a line plot.

Engineering: Agricultural Engineering

Types of Engineering for Kids' Exploration

A STEM career field to which students can be introduced in this project is Environmental Engineering, which can include climate and atmospheric science. Scan the QR code to read more about the field of environmental engineering.

To engage children in developmentally appropriate engineering design aligned with elementary science and engineering standards, have children create a weather station of their own. If they have access to instruments such as a thermometer or barometer, they can include those in their weather station. Two more accessible possibilities are a homemade weather vane and/or anemometer to measure wind. Children can use cups, dowels or rigid straws, and a pencil to construct a homemade version of the anemometer shown in Figure 5.5. Similar materials plus paper and scissors can be used to design a weather vane.

Figure 5.5 Children can engineer their own version of an anemometer to measure wind speed.

While teachers or families can look up examples of homemade weather instruments, it is important that children have a chance to engage in the engineering design process to create an instrument that shows the direction and/or speed of wind. To support engineering standards, scaffold the learning by encouraging children to collect ideas and discuss their plans before building a prototype. Above all, ensure that children are the ones engaged in planning and experimentation, rather than providing a predetermined list of steps to follow.

NGSS Engineering Design Standards

The engineering design challenge in this chapter provides opportunities for children to develop understanding of the NGSS Engineering Design Standards identified here.

K–2 ACTIVITIES	3–5 ACTIVITIES
K-2-ETS1-2. Develop a simple sketch, drawing, or physical model to illustrate how the shape of an object helps it function as needed to solve a given problem.	**3-5-ETS1-1.** Define a simple design problem reflecting a need or a want that includes specified criteria for success and constraints on materials, time, or cost.

Extensions and Connections

Entertainment. Movies and television programs involving weather can supplement the activities in this project. Movies about weather rated G or PG include Disney's *Frozen* and *Frozen 2*, as well as the *Ice Age* movie series which incorporate climate change concepts. Some children's programs about weather are *The Magic School Bus* "Kicks up a Storm" episode or the *Sid the Science Kid* "Sid the Weatherman" episode.

Children's Literature. Weather is the topic of many fiction and nonfiction children's books. Choosing weather-themed books during this project supports both reading and the content of the activities. Some possible titles include *Cloudy with a Chance of Meatballs* by Judi Barrett, *Thunder Cake* by Patricia Polacco, *Little Cloud* by Eric Carle, *Come on, Rain!* by Karen Hesse, and *Fly Guy Presents: Weather* by Tedd Arnold. Other books about weather that children have at home or check out from the library can also complement this project.

Writing. In preparing for their weather forecasts, children could write scripts. Alternatively, children could write a story about a day with perfect weather. Such a story would invite kids to bring in aspects of their own identity, think about the weather they prefer, and describe weather in ways that demonstrate some of the scientific understanding in this project.

Social Studies. As children learn about climate in regions around the world, they can also explore the geography, history, and culture of the regions they select. Children could create maps of the regions they select or present what they learn in person, in writing, or using technology within online school. Topics such as these could also serve as topics of dinner conversation.

Fine Arts. A common weather-related art project for young children involves creating clouds with paper, glue, and cotton balls. Creating visual artwork of landscapes with rain can be a challenge for older children. This project might also be connected with learning about the rain dance rituals and traditions of indigenous peoples in North America.

Computer Science. Children with access to BBC micro:bit, littleBits, or Raspberry Pi computing devices could program them to be part of the weather data station they create in the engineering design challenge. If a child has access to Cubelets modular robotics, they could use the temperature and light sensing blocks as part of a weather data station design, as well.

Short Circuit

In most contexts, children are told not to play with electricity and warned of its dangers. Although precautions must always be taken, this chapter offers safe methods of exploration and learning opportunities focused around the theme of circuits and electricity. Through these activities, children will engage in hands-on exploration of circuits, with a focus on materials that conduct electricity. While math involved in electricity and circuits is often too advanced for young students, this chapter offers age-appropriate math activities by demonstrating how to use circuit drawings to understand shapes, learning more about circuits in the process. The engineering design challenge combines the ideas in the science and math sections, showing how to create circuits using household materials.

ISTE Standards for Students

The uses of technology in this chapter are most aligned with the following ISTE Standards for Students. Some of the technology learning opportunities in this chapter are specific to science and math content. Students can also use many technologies to present and share their learning. Tools such as discussion boards and student-generated multimedia presentations (e.g., podcasts or videos) could be used to support technology learning regardless of specific math or science content.

Empowered Learner

1c. Students use technology to seek feedback that informs and improves their practice and to demonstrate their learning in a variety of ways.

Knowledge Constructor

3d. Students build knowledge by actively exploring real-world issues and problems, developing ideas and theories and pursuing answers and solutions.

Innovative Designer

4a. Students know and use a deliberate design process for generating ideas, testing theories, creating innovative artifacts or solving authentic problems.

4d. Students exhibit a tolerance for ambiguity, perseverance and the capacity to work with open-ended problems

Computational Thinker

5c. Students break problems into component parts, extract key information, and develop descriptive models to understand complex systems or facilitate problem-solving.

Materials, Time, and Supervision

Because electricity is all around us, it is a phenomenon that children can explore in many contexts. Consistent with other projects in this book, most children should be able to finish the activities in this chapter in about a week or two. The exact length of time will depend on children's prior knowledge; specific activities that teachers, families, and children select; and curriculum connections that may extend learning beyond the suggestions in this chapter. Although suggested activities are generally safe for children, adults are encouraged to monitor children closely as they work with batteries and electricity.

Minimum materials needed for activities in this chapter include items listed in Table 6.1.

TABLE 6.1 Project Materials

REQUIRED MATERIALS
• Connected device (laptop, desktop, tablet, or smartphone)
• Potato, lemon, apple, other fruits or vegetables of similar sizes
• Galvanized (zinc) nails
• Conductive wire (copper works best)
• Pennies or copper nail
• Light bulb (the smaller the better)
• Small device that operates with AA, C, or D batteries (e.g., flashlight, remote, inexpensive children's toy)
• AAA battery
• Foil and materials such as fabric, paper, wax paper, or plastic.
• Binder clips and paper clips
• LED tea light

Resources to Explore and Inspire

Throughout this project, children will engage in hands-on exploration of circuits. To get started or to support during or after exploration, a number of websites introduce concepts of electricity, energy, safety, and circuits. Table 6.2 summarizes online resources teachers and families might use to introduce the context of the activity, extend learning, and incorporate after science explorations to expand on scientific ideas.

TABLE 6.2 Resources to Explore: Short Circuit

RESOURCE	DESCRIPTION	GRADE LEVEL	CODE
Electric Choice	Facts, glossary, safety tips, myths, and history of electricity, including renewable and nonrenewable sources.	K–5	qrgo.page.link/RSzQR
Energy Kids from U.S. Energy Information Administration	Lesson plans, experiments, field trips, career information, and related resource links about electricity and energy.	K–5	qrgo.page.link/XcXFm
Electrical Safety Foundation International	Elementary educational resources including lessons, learning materials, student printouts, and games about electricity and safety.	3–5	qrgo.page.link/u4KKi
Learning Circuits	Website with self-paced, animated tutorials, diagrams, and quizzes about circuits.	3–5	bit.ly/383IQL1

Science: Electricity

The science focus in this lesson emphasizes materials and relationships that conduct electricity. Children will explore which materials conduct electricity and which do not.

NGSS Disciplinary Core Ideas for Science

Science learning in this chapter aligns with the standards shown here. The standards emphasize *analyzing, asking questions, observing,* and *providing evidence.* Children can deepen their understanding of these standards through hands-on explorations and discussion to unpack the concepts they discover.

K–2 ACTIVITIES	3–5 ACTIVITIES
2-PS1-2. Analyze data obtained from testing different materials to determine which materials have the properties that are best suited for an intended purpose.	**3-PS2-3.** Ask questions to determine cause and effect relationships of electric or magnetic interactions between two objects not in contact with each other. **4-PS3-2.** Make observations to provide evidence that energy can be transferred from place to place by sound, light, heat, and electric currents.

Getting Started

To learn about electricity, children can build and test circuits consisting mostly of common household items; many adults may be familiar with potato lights or similar projects, for example. Building a circuit is a valuable learning experience, but experimenting and reasoning about the scientific phenomenon that makes the circuit work (or not) invites deeper science learning.

Before students begin testing materials to determine which do or do not conduct electricity, ask them to predict which ones they think will work and why. After testing each item, record the result. Recording observations in a table or organized list can help children notice patterns among objects and also offers evidence that children can use to strengthen their explanations. Early readers can use drawings or images of different materials and record simple yes/no data. After experimenting, engage children in discussion to elicit what they think and build upon their observations. Possible questions include:

- How do your predictions compare with the results?

- What patterns do you notice?

- Why do you think it works with this material but not that one?

- What is it about this material that makes the bulb light up?

- What do you think would happen if we chose a big light bulb instead of this small one?

- What other materials could we test?

Recording and analyzing data, comparing and contrasting results, observing patterns, and discovering cause-and-effect relationships support both the science content students are learning, as well as some of the crosscutting concepts that span across disciplinary boundaries.

Grade-Level Guidelines

Both experiments in this chapter invite children to test multiple objects or materials to determine the extent to which they conduct electricity. The depth and level of sophistication for the discussions that follow the activities depend on the student's grade level and prior knowledge.

Grades K–2

Young learners can explore electricity and early concepts of conductivity by beginning with a classic science fair project: building a potato lamp. Using just a potato, pennies (or copper nails), galvanized (zinc) nails, wire, and a small light bulb, children may be amazed to see a bulb light up. To construct the potato lamp with young children:

1. Help the child cut the potato in half and make slits to hold a penny in each.

2. Have the child help wrap copper wire around the pennies (leaving several inches of wire protruding from the pennies)

3. Have the child insert the pennies into the slits in each side of the potato.

4. With your supervision, have the child wrap wire around one of the zinc nails and stick it into one of the potato halves.

5. Next, use some of the wire connected to one of the pennies and wrap it around the other nail, then stick the nail in the other potato half.

6. Connect the loose ends of the wires to the base of a small light bulb, ensuring metal-to-metal contact between the wire and light bulb base. (When working with young children, adults should do this step.)

How to Make a
Potato-Powered
Light Bulb

If a low-power bulb is not available, consider another small electrical device. Figure 6.1 shows a potato battery that powers a basic calculator instead of a light. For a more detailed explanation of how to build a potato lamp, scan the QR code here.

After building a potato lamp, discuss why and how the potato made the bulb light up. Electricity runs through the wires and to the bulb, but where does the electricity come from? And what is the potato doing? The sugar, water, and acid in the potato reacts with the metal of the pennies and nails. Chemical energy is transferred to electrical energy, creating a small electrical current that powers the light bulb. The full description may not be accessible to very young learners, but essentially, the potato and metals act as a battery to power the light bulb. Inquisitive young children may wonder if other foods can be batteries too.

At this point, students can engage in more experimentation by trying to make the same device with foods other than a potato. Lemons and other highly acidic fruits work well. What about apples? Zucchini? Tomatoes? Onions? It is at this point that children should make predictions and record which foods result in the bulb lighting up and which do not. Children may wonder why some foods work while others do not. As students test and analyze materials to discover which ones light up the bulb, what they are really exploring is which foods are conductive. While children will not likely know the word "conductive," they may be able to describe the phenomenon using phrases such as, "electricity goes through it" and can be introduced to the word during discussion of what students noticed and wondered.

Figure 6.1 This image shows a potato battery powering a calculator.

Grades 3–5

Children in later grades can also explore conductivity, electric interactions, and electric current. Older students may enjoy building and experimenting with the same potato and fruit/vegetable lamps previously described. While younger children focus on which materials are best suited for conducting electricity, discussion with older children doing the same activity should emphasize energy transfer and electric current.

Another way that older students can learn about electric interactions involves powering a small object with batteries of different sizes (Figure 6.2). You'll need a flashlight, toy, or battery pack that normally uses a size C or D battery; a AAA or AA battery; foil; and other materials such as fabric, paper, wax paper, and plastic. Ask the child to consider whether they think a smaller battery could substitute for one of the larger batteries and why or why not?

Figure 6.2 The common batteries shown here are different sizes, but all have the same 1.5V voltage.

In order for the battery to work, it must touch both ends of the receptacle and complete a circuit. Although smaller batteries will not fit in a way that completes the circuit, students can investigate materials that could complete the circuit. If a conductive material is placed at one end of the battery and touches the end of the cartridge or receptacle, then a smaller 1.5V battery can be substituted for a larger one. Depending on the shape and size of the battery-operated device, children could try aluminum foil, coins, plastic, cloth, paper, or other safe substances to discover which ones are conductive enough to make a smaller battery work in place of a larger one. Of course, adult supervision is essential to ensure safety during this investigation.

There are a number of products and STEM toys on the market that focus on circuits and electricity, such as Snap Circuits, Squishy Circuits, and Circuit Clay. There are also paper circuits made from conductive copper tape, LEDs, and coin cell batteries. Options such as these can be excellent opportunities for children to learn about electricity and circuits, but they can be cost prohibitive and inaccessible for many children. Table 6.3 summarizes some free, online resources that support children's science learning related to electricity and circuits.

TABLE 6.3 Science Resources for Electricity Activities

RESOURCE	DESCRIPTION	GRADE LEVEL	CODE
Frankenstein's Lightning Laboratory	A series of electricity-related projects for kids.	K–5	qrgo.page.link/Jx3eR
ScienceWiz	Interactive activities, animations, and extensions focused on sub-topics of electricity.	K–5	qrgo.page.link/PxTm3
PBS Learning Electric Circuits	Lesson plan with hands-on activities.	3–5	qrgo.page.link/bFgcb
PhET Science Simulations	Interactive online simulations including balloons and static electricity, circuit construction, magnets and compass or electromagnets, and "John Travoltage."	3–5	qrgo.page.link/P5ufr

Math: Exploring Shape

Electricity and circuits certainly involve mathematics, but much of the math is far too advanced for elementary students. With some creativity, even young learners can still explore mathematics in the context of electricity and even learn more about circuits as they do so.

CCSSM Math Content Standards

Extending this chapter's science investigation invites math learning about shape and geometry. Math activities in this project support math standards in K–5, as shown here.

K-2 ACTIVITIES	3-5 ACTIVITIES
CCSS.MATH.CONTENT.1.G.A.2. Compose two-dimensional shapes (rectangles, squares, trapezoids, triangles, half-circles, and quarter-circles) or three-dimensional shapes (cubes, right rectangular prisms, right circular cones, and right circular cylinders) to create a composite shape, and compose new shapes from the composite shape. **CCSS.MATH.CONTENT.2.GA.1.** Recognize and draw shapes having specified attributes, such as a given number of angles or a given number of equal faces. Identify triangles, quadrilaterals, pentagons, hexagons, and cubes.	**CCSS.MATH.CONTENT.4.G.A.1.** Draw points, lines, line segments, rays, angles (right, acute, obtuse), and perpendicular and parallel lines. Identify these in two-dimensional figures. **CCSS.MATH.CONTENT.4.G.A.3.** Recognize a line of symmetry for a two-dimensional figure as a line across the figure such that the figure can be folded along the line into matching parts. Identify line-symmetric figures and draw lines of symmetry.

Getting Started

Although elementary students learning about electricity may not typically work with formal circuit diagrams, introducing them in this project creates an opportunity for age-appropriate math learning and extends science learning. Circuit diagrams provide a relevant context for learning about two-dimensional shapes and their attributes, lines and angles, and symmetry.

Many children "learn their shapes" at a young age. Identifying shapes in early grades seems fairly simplistic, but there is more than meets the eye. It is important that children see shapes in a variety of orientations, sizes, and types. For instance, Figure 6.3 shows a variety of shapes. The image shows several triangles, yet children are surprisingly likely to identify only triangles that are equilateral with one side horizontal (Shape B). Similarly, children may recognize trapezoids such as Shape E, but not realize that Shape G is also a trapezoid—even high school and college students sometimes struggle with this! Focusing on the attributes and definitions of shapes helps students develop greater mathematical understanding. In other words, a triangle isn't a shape that "looks like" Shape B; it is a polygon with three edges and three vertices. And Shapes E and G are both trapezoids because they are quadrilaterals with exactly one pair of parallel sides. Emphasizing attributes and definitions of shapes lends itself to later work with classifying quadrilaterals, when many children struggle to understand that squares are always rectangles, but rectangles aren't always squares.

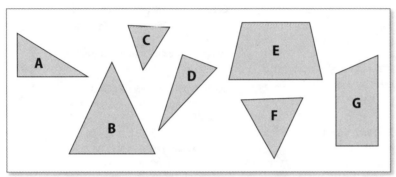

Figure 6.3 Understanding the attributes of shapes, like those shown here, can help children build an understanding of circuit diagrams, further extending math and science learning.

Grade-Level Guidelines

The mathematical goals of the following activities align with math standards for grades K–2 and grades 3–5. Circuit diagrams (Figure 6.4) provide a context and connection to the science students learn during prior activities. However, the content is much more advanced than the grade-level science standards would suggest. Teachers and families can acknowledge this by telling children that the pictures are diagrams that electricians, scientists, and engineers use to plan and understand more complicated circuits. Each symbol in the diagram indicates something about the circuit.

Figure 6.4 can be used to connect this chapter's hands-on elementary science activities with the mathematics activities. Showing the side-by-side images, ask children to compare what they see and try to figure out which symbol represents the lamp, which represents the switch, and which represents the battery or voltage source. Students may figure this out for themselves or may need some additional prompting, especially since the locations of the components are different in the two images. They may draw lines from the lamp to the corresponding symbol (circle with an X in it), from the voltage source to its symbol (perhaps noticing the − and +), and draw a line between the switch and symbol which looks similar and is in the same position in the images. These symbols represent a simple circuit, but many circuits are not simple. Challenge students to think of how complicated a diagram might look for their whole house or school, perhaps doing an internet search for "circuit diagram for a house." Introducing the math activities in this way may help students to connect with science without overwhelming them with science content that is beyond their level of understanding.

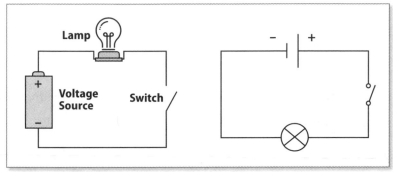

Figure 6.4 Explain to children that circuit diagrams like those shown here are used to plan and understand more complicated circuits.

Grades K–2

Ironically, the math activity for K–2 students involves more advanced circuit diagrams than for grades 3–5. Since the mathematical purpose is to identify various shapes and describe their attributes, we need sophisticated diagrams that include a variety of symbols.

Begin by showing students a key of electronic circuit symbols, such as Figure 6.5, or a similar image you could display online or in an online course. Ask students to search the image for the following shapes: circle, rectangle, triangle, and trapezoid. Table 6.4 summarizes where these shapes are located within Figure 6.5 and the challenges and misconceptions children may face when trying to identify them in the image. Each misconception offers an opportunity for children to focus on the attributes and definition of each shape—what does it mean for a shape to be a circle, rectangle, triangle, or trapezoid?

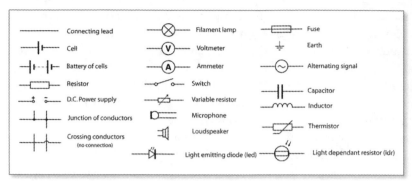

Figure 6.5 Use a key of electronic circuit symbols, like those shown here, to help students understand shapes and their attributes.

TABLE 6.4 Shapes Within Circuit Diagram Symbols

SHAPE	SYMBOLS INCLUDING THE SHAPE	ANTICIPATED STUDENT MISCONCEPTIONS
Circle	D.C. power supply Filament lamp Voltmeter Ammeter Switch Microphone Alternating signal Light-dependent resistor (LDR)	• Students may not notice the small circles in the D.C. power supply and switch images. • Students may argue that one end of the microphone symbol is flat, so it is not truly a circle. • Students may notice that the inductor symbol looks like half circles.
Rectangle	Resistor Variable resistor Loudspeaker Fuse Thermistor Light-dependent resistor (LDR)	• Students may not see the small rectangle in the loudspeaker symbol, particularly because it is the only one that is vertically positioned. • Students may argue that the ends of the rectangle inside the light-dependent resistor symbol are rounded, therefore not truly a rectangle.
Triangle	Light-emitting diode (LED)	• Students may see each region in the filament lamp symbol as a triangle.
Trapezoid	Variable resistor Loudspeaker Thermistor	• Students may struggle to identify the loudspeaker trapezoid because is vertically oriented and small. • Students may struggle to identify the trapezoids in the variable resistor and thermistor because they are used to seeing symmetrical trapezoids.

A logical extension of identifying shapes within a table of symbols is to identify shapes within actual electrical circuit diagrams. A quick online search will yield many images of electrical circuit diagrams (or schematics) to use for this activity. Be mindful that these diagrams can be quite complicated, show symbols not shown in Figure 6.5, or include writing that may be distracting to students. Also anticipate that some children will want to make sense of the diagram. Trying to associate the symbols in Figure 6.5 with what they see in Figure 6.6 can be a great way for kids to connect across representations and make sense of the context of their math activity. However, more sophisticated diagrams may have so many unfamiliar symbols and terms that matching symbols could become a source of frustration.

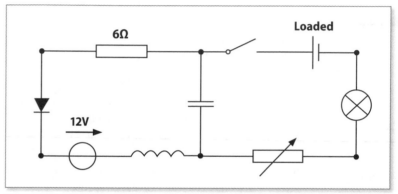

Figure 6.6 Students can practice identifying shapes in an actual electrical circuit diagram, like the one shown here.

Grades 3–5

Geometry of shapes in later elementary grades focuses more on lines, angles, and symmetry than simply identifying shapes. Children could be asked to analyze images such as Figure 6.6 to identify acute, obtuse, and right angles, parallel and perpendicular lines, or lines of symmetry. This particular image provides a good opportunity to find multiple examples of parallel and perpendicular lines, right angles, acute angles within the triangle symbol or variable resistor, and obtuse angles at the switch and also within the variable resistor symbol. Students who have been learning about rays and line segments may also notice similarities between the mathematical representations for rays and line segments and images they see in the circuit diagram.

You might also think to ask children to draw their own diagrams with specific conditions (e.g., four right angles, two pairs of parallel lines, and one obtuse angle),

Figure 6.7 Use a diagram like this one to help students understand concepts such as parallel lines.

but I do not advise this because the result could be a nonsensical circuit diagram that is scientifically inaccurate. Working with diagrams that are more advanced than students' current understanding is one thing, but we do not want to encourage scientific misinformation.

You can preview more advanced science content as you highlight mathematical content that is grade-level appropriate. As students learn about parallel lines, you can connect this to the idea of parallel circuits. Show an image such as Figure 6.7, and ask the child why they think this is called a "parallel circuit". Students are likely to notice that the three lightbulbs are on parallel lines.

You might also challenge students to figure out which of the circuits shown in Figure 6.8 is called a parallel circuit. They are likely to notice that the image on the left has more parallel lines and/ or bulbs that are located on lines that are parallel to one another. The image on the right (a series circuit) also has two sets of parallel lines—a vertical pair and a horizontal pair—but the bulbs are not located parallel to one another. To bring in the mathematical idea of symmetry, children can be asked to find lines of symmetry for any of the electrical circuit diagrams or symbols.

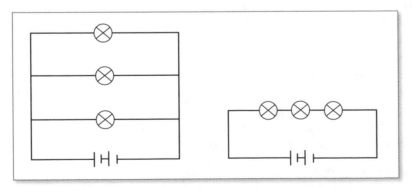

Figure 6.8 You can use images like this to help students identify parallel circuits.

TABLE 6.5 Mathematics Resources for Exploring Shape Activities

RESOURCE	DESCRIPTION	GRADE LEVEL	CODE
Circuit Diagram	User-friendly online circuit diagram creator adults could use to make images for K–5 children to analyze for shapes.	K–5	qrgo.page.link/k3xbb
NCTM Shape Tool	Interactive tool to create and manipulate two-dimensional geometric shapes.	K–5	qrgo.page.link/nddMc
Teach Engineering Lesson	Circuits: One Path for Electricity lesson is aligned to NGSS and math standards. It focuses on series circuits and circuit diagram representations.	3–5	qrgo.page.link/LirwK

Engineering: Electrical Engineering

Electrical engineering is an obvious engineering connection for this project. Electrical engineers work with other engineers in fields such as energy, consumer electronics, and telecommunications. The work of electrical engineers touches children's everyday lives in many ways. Scan the QR code to learn more about the field of electrical engineering and explore engineering curriculum ideas for kids.

Types of Engineering for Kids' Exploration

In this project, students learned about conductivity through science activities and about circuit diagrams through math activities. The engineering design challenge combines these ideas, allowing students to create their own circuits using household materials. Using cardboard, binder and paper clips, an LED tealight candle, a coin cell battery, and aluminum foil, children will create circuits with a variety of switch types in order to light up an LED bulb.

As part of the planning phase of the engineering design process, children can create their own simple circuit diagrams with switches, batteries, and LED lights. Up to this point, "switch" has been used as a generic term. Children can consider the types of switches they know. They may identify dial switches such as dimmers, clip switches such as normal household light switches, or push switches which only work while being pushed, similar to the potato lamp circuit.

MAKE PROJECTS:
Scrappy Circuits

Scan the QR code for a detailed explanation for how to make these Scrappy Circuits (Carroll, 2019). Adults should provide constant supervision as children create and engage with this activity, to ensure safety. However, children can build, test, and improve the circuits they imagined and planned on paper. The LED light offers a simple criterion for success—either it lights up or it doesn't!

NGSS Engineering Design Standards

The engineering design challenge in this chapter provides opportunities for children to develop understanding of the NGSS Engineering Design Standards identified here.

K-2 ACTIVITIES	3-5 ACTIVITIES
K-2-ETS1-3. Develop a simple sketch, drawing, or physical model to illustrate how the shape of an object helps it function as needed to solve a given problem.	**3-5-ETS1-2.** Generate and compare multiple possible solutions to a problem based on how well each is likely to meet the criteria and constraints of the problem.

Extensions and Connections

Entertainment. Movies that connect with ideas about electricity include the film *Short Circuit* (rated PG by 1980s U.S. standards), *Monsters, Inc.*, or *Meet the Robinsons*. *The Magic School Bus* series focuses on electricity in the "Gets Charged" episode in Season 4, and *Sid the Science Kid* explores electricity in the "Let There Be Light" episode. Children who play *Minecraft* are likely already familiar with Redstone, which is the game's equivalent of electricity. Ask kids how they use Redstone in *Minecraft* and how they can connect the idea of circuits with what they build and do in the game.

Children's Literature. Children's books are an excellent way for kids to learn more about electricity and develop reading skills. Possible titles for this project include: *Charged Up: The Story of Electricity* by Jacqui Bailey, *Switch On, Switch Off* by Melvin Berger, Joanna Cole's *The Magic School Bus and the Electric Field Trip*, and *Oscar and the Bird: A Book about Electricity* by Geoff Waring. These are but a few of the options available for teachers and families to connect STEM learning with reading.

Social Studies. Extend what children learn about electricity and circuits by examining historical figures and events. Critical comparison of the lives and contributions of Thomas Edison, Hertha Ayrton, or Nikola Tesla can involve creating timelines of their lives and major events, learning about the war of the currents in the late 1880s United States, and researching the 1893 Chicago World's Fair.

Computer Science. A variety of STEM-focused tools and toys can engage children with electricity and circuits. For example, littleBits and Makey Makey each allow children of all ages to safely explore ideas about circuits as they use their imaginations to create and invent projects.

Fine Arts. With a battery, LED lights, and copper tape, children can make paper circuits that will illuminate any drawing or piece of artwork. A quick online search of "paper circuits" will yield ideas and directions for how to use circuits to transform children's artwork. Paper circuit materials can be a great addition to a maker space, too.

Physical Education. Create an age-appropriate circuit training challenge for children to have fun exercising at several different stations, each with a different activity. Though circuit training in fitness is not specifically related to electricity, challenge children to figure out why they might call it "circuits." Just as electricity follows a path in a circuit, so too does a person who exercises at a series of stations.

Catching the Vibe
with Sound Waves

S ound can be an interesting concept for children, once they really think about it. They can't see it, but most of them can hear it. Hearing sound helps keep us safe when we cross the street, gives us the gift of music, and can even help us navigate in the world. But **how** do we hear sound? In these projects, children will be able to see the vibrations that the brain interprets as sound. Older students will be introduced to some basic terminology to describe sound waves, including frequency, amplitude, and decibels. Connections will be made between sound, music, and mathematics; and as an extension, children will discover the sound-based navigation technique that bats and other animals—and even some humans—employ.

ISTE Standards for Students

The technology suggestions embedded throughout this project advance students toward the ISTE standards identified below. Additional ISTE standards can be addressed through supplemental activities and the use of technology tools for communicating, presenting, and assessing in an online schooling environment.

Knowledge Constructor

3c. Students curate information from digital resources using a variety of tools and methods to create collections of artifacts that demonstrate meaningful connections or conclusions.

3d. Students build knowledge by actively exploring real-world issues and problems, developing ideas and theories and pursuing answers and solutions.

Innovative Designer

4c. Students develop, test and refine prototypes as part of a cyclical design process.

Materials, Time, and Supervision

Because sound is all around us, it is a phenomenon that children can explore in many contexts. Most children should be able to finish the activities in this chapter in less than a week. The exact length of time will depend on children's prior knowledge; specific activities that teachers, families, and children select; and curriculum connections that may extend learning beyond the suggestions in this chapter. Although suggested activities are generally safe for children, adults are encouraged to monitor children closely as they work with electronic speakers as well as glass bowls and bottles.

To engage with these projects, students will need access to the materials listed in Table 7.1. Various options are provided so families can tailor the project to their child and the materials they have available.

TABLE 7.1 Project Materials

GRADE K–5 MATERIALS	GRADE 3–5 MATERIALS
• Music speaker or large radio	• 6 identical test tubes or 6 identical glass bottles
• Aluminum (or similar) cookie pan or cake sheet	• Test tube rack (if using test tubes)
• Dry, uncooked rice	• Water
• Metal pencil or pen	• Metal pencil or pen, or metal spoon
• Metal water bottle	• Several types of string, yarn, fishing line (30 ft ea.)
• Roll of paper towels	• Several sizes of paper cups (2 of each size)
• Wine glass half full of water	
• Athletic shoe	
• Large empty bowl	
• Cellophane wrap	
• Shoebox (or similar)	
• 2 fat markers	
• String (30 feet)	
• 2 paper cups	

Resources to Explore and Inspire

Throughout this project, children will engage in hands-on exploration of how sound works. To get started or to support during or after exploration, many web-based resources can be used to introduce concepts of sound transmission, vibrations, and waveform. Table 7.2 summarizes online resources teachers and families might use to introduce the context of the activity, extend learning, and incorporate after the project to expand on scientific ideas.

TABLE 7.2 Resources to Explore: Catching the Vibe with Sound Waves

RESOURCE	DESCRIPTION	GRADE LEVEL	CODE
Science Wiz: Bouncy Balls	The Bouncy Balls application enables children to "see" sound with various-sized balls that move in reaction to sounds and speech.	K–5	bit.ly/376ldlz
American Acoustical Society: Explore Sound	A variety of projects and activities. Acoustics at Home is perfect for distance learners.	K–5	bit.ly/2JWjLJL
PhET Interactive Simulations: Sound and Wave Simulations	Three terrific sound and wave simulations allow children to visualize how sound waves travel.	K–5	bit.ly/3bjXqBd
SkyPaw: Decibel X Pro Noise Meter	A free downloadable app that measures the sound level all around you.	3–5	bit.ly/2Kh9IyE
PBS LearningMedia: Sound Waves	Excellent videos and interactive lessons about sound waves.	Varies for each video and lesson	bit.ly/3ndaNqc

(Continued)

RESOURCE	DESCRIPTION	GRADE LEVEL	CODE
Exploratorium	Dozens of engaging projects demonstrating different aspects of sound.	K–5	bit.ly/37Ry1LN
Fizzics Education: Light & Sound Experiments	Interesting educational projects with step-by-step instructions.	3–5	bit.ly/3oB54KM

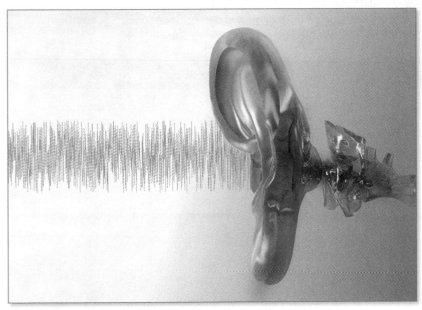

Figure 7.1 Sound waves enter the ear to be interpreted by the brain.

Science: The Basics of Sound

In a nutshell, what our brain interprets as sound is simply vibrations that travel in waves. Usually, these vibrations travel as waves from their source, through the air, and into our ears, where our brain then interprets them as sound (Figure 7.1). These vibrations can also travel as waves through liquids and solids, and into our ears. To describe these vibrations, we use basic terminology such as frequency, amplitude, and decibels.

NGSS Disciplinary Core Ideas for Science

Science learning in this chapter aligns with the standards shown here. The standards emphasize actively engaging in science, including verbs such as *plan* and *conduct*. Thus, it is especially important that children have opportunities to do hands-on science—construct and experiment, make observations, and conduct investigations—as well as discuss their scientific thinking with teachers, peers, or family members.

K-2 ACTIVITIES	3-5 ACTIVITIES
1-PS4-1. Plan and conduct investigations to provide evidence that vibrating materials can make sound and that sound can make materials vibrate. **2-PS1-1.** Plan and conduct an investigation to describe and classify different kinds of materials by their observable properties.	**4-PS4-1.** Develop a model of waves to describe patterns in terms of amplitude and wavelength and that waves can cause objects to move.

Getting Started

To learn about sound, vibration, and waves, it helps to give children a way to visualize what is happening. They can do this through experiments using mostly common household items. Have your K–5 student complete the vibrating rice project in either Kids Academy (first half of video) or Cool Science Experiments in Table 6.3. (They are basically the same experiment; choose which one to complete based on what materials you have available.)

TABLE 7.3 Science Resources for The Basics of Sound Activities

RESOURCE	DESCRIPTION	GRADE LEVEL	CODE
Kids Academy: Sound Experiments for Kids	A video giving a very basic explanation of what sound is.	K–5	bit.ly/3768Y8P
Cool Science Experiments Headquarters: How to See Sound Science Experiment	A basic demonstration that shows the vibrations that create sound.	K–5	bit.ly/33Y1um3
KClassScienceChannel: Length of Rubber Band Determines Pitch	An easy-to-follow video showing a simple project that demonstrates frequency (or pitch).	K–5	bit.ly/3oEJUvj
Scholastic Study Jams: Sound	Engaging video covering all sound basics, including vibrations, waves, frequency, amplitude, and decibels.	3–5	bit.ly/3n7C8Kg
Home Science Tools: Test Tube Xylophone	Video instructions for making a test-tube liquid xylophone and a discussion of pitch (frequency).	3–5	bit.ly/3acLp07
Peekaboo Kidz: The Dr. Binocs Show, What Is Sound?	Video covering all sound basics, including vibrations, waves, frequency, pitch, decibels, and what happens to sound in a vacuum.	K–5	bit.ly/2KSYOji

After the children see the experiment's results of the rice vibrating due to a nearby sound source, take a moment to discuss some questions, such as:

- The pan holding the rice (or the bowl with cellophane wrap) is not touching the sound source. What is causing the rice to vibrate?

- Did you expect the rice to vibrate?

- Is the sound source vibrating?

- What else is vibrating?

- Do you think the rice would vibrate if all the air was sucked out of the room?

Discovering cause and effect relationships supports both the science content students are learning, as well as some of the crosscutting concepts that span across disciplinary boundaries.

Grade-Level Guidelines

Here are grade-appropriate experiments to explore more aspects of sound.

Grades K–2

The following grade K–2 experiments allow children to observe a phenomenon and then make predictions. The depth and level of sophistication for the discussions that follow the activities depend on the student's grade level and prior knowledge.

Watch the second half of the Kids Academy video in Table 7.3, where the demonstrator shows how different materials vibrate and emit sound, or else absorb vibrations and emit very little sound. Discuss what it is about different materials that makes them vibrate versus absorbing vibrations. Have children gather other objects and guess whether they will vibrate or absorb vibrations. See if their predictions hold true.

Watch the KClassScienceChannel video and construct the rubber-band-and-shoebox project. Place the two fat markers under the stretched rubber band at different widths apart and have students guess whether the pitch will be higher or lower than the previous pitch. Discuss different stringed instruments and make connections to your simple shoebox instrument.

Grades 3–5

The following grade 3–5 experiment allows children to make predictions using prior knowledge.

Older children should be exposed to basic sound terminology. Play the Scholastic Study Jams video in Table 7.3.

- Review the concept of frequency: more waves per second results in higher pitch; fewer waves per second results in lower pitch.

- Review the concept of amplitude: bigger waves result in louder sounds; smaller waves result in quieter sounds.

- Review the concept of decibels: decibels are a unit of measure for amplitude (loudness).

Now have students complete the Home Science Tools: Test Tube Xylophone project in Table 7.3 (groups may split into pairs or trios). Remember that identical glass bottles (or identical glass containers of any kind) will likely work as well as test tubes. Once completed, ask the students:

- Does the amount of water in each container allow you to predict whether that container will vibrate at a higher or lower frequency? Explain your thinking.

- Can you cause one of your containers to emit the pitch "middle C" (found either on a piano, or do a search for websites that play middle C for you). How do you plan to accomplish this?

Math: Musical Connections

Music and math have an integral relationship. The pitch of a musical note can be expressed mathematically, and so can the rhythms of music. Research has shown that students who learn to read and play music tend to have stronger math skills than those who do not.

CCSSM Math Content Standards

Many mathematics connections are possible within the music context. The basic math activity in this project supports math standards in grades 3–5, as shown here. The advanced activity (exponential curve) is a good introduction to graphing points on x and y axes (usually taught in middle school); graphing and understanding exponential curves is not usually taught until high school. The very advanced activity (decibels) is a good introduction to logarithmic logic, not usually taught until pre-calculus.

K–2 ACTIVITIES	3–5 ACTIVITIES
CCSS.MATH.CONTENT.K.MD.A.2. Directly compare two objects with a measurable attribute in common, to see which object has "more of"/"less of" the attribute, and describe the difference.	**CCSS.MATH.CONTENT.3.OA.A.4.** Determine the unknown whole number in a multiplication or division equation relating three whole numbers. **CCSS.MATH.CONTENT.4.OA.C.5.** Generate a number or shape pattern that follows a given rule. **CCSS.MATH.CONTENT.5.NF.B.4.** Apply and extend previous understandings of multiplication to multiply a fraction or whole number by a fraction.

Getting Started

The math activities in this section involve exploring pitch, which can vary depending on how fast an object vibrates. These activities are featured in the Chrome Music Lab (see each one for details).

Grade-Level Guidelines

The activities in this chapter are grouped according to K–2 and 3–5 grade bands.

Sound Waves

Grades K–2

Scan the QR code to access the Sound Waves activity for grades K–2.

Play a low note on the keyboard, and ask students to describe the way the air molecules (illustrated with blue dots) move.

- Are they moving slow or fast?

- What happens when you play a high note?

- Are they moving faster or slower than the low note?

- Zoom in using the magnifying glass in the bottom-right corner, and play a low note. Hold down on the note to create the waveform. Describe the waveform of a low note. Play a high note and describe the waveform now—is it different from the low note?

Strings

Grades 3–5

Scan the QR code to access the activity for grades 3–5, which explains how pitch can be changed through adjusting the vibration on the strings of an instrument such as a guitar.

Play two notes exactly one octave apart for your students. Ask them to notice how the two notes sound the same, except one is higher and one is lower.

Have students play the notes for each length of string. Ask students to describe what they notice.

- What is the relationship between the length of the string segment and the pitch of the note?

- If you change the length of the string, what happens to the sound?

In his paper *Mathematical Harmonies* (2001), researcher Mark Petersen explains how frequency, or pitch, can be changed in three ways, as shown in Figure 7.2.

HOW TO CHANGE FREQUENCY OR PITCH

Tighten the string: ⬆ tension   results in: ⬆ frequency

Use a thicker string: ⬆ line density   results in: ⬇ frequency

Use fingers on frets: ⬇ length   results in: ⬆ frequency

Figure 7.2 You can change the frequency by tightening or loosening a string, changing the thickness of a string, or changing the position of your fingers on the frets of a guitar (the vertical lines on the guitar's neck).

Ask students if they have noticed the following:

- Instruments that play low notes are much larger than high instruments. For example, look at the string family. The violin is the smallest. The viola is only a little larger, the cello is large, and the bass is very large.

- Have you ever noticed the organ pipes at the front of a church? Organ pipes double in size to go down an octave.

- Frets are far apart at the neck and close together near the body.

Review that sound is made up of waves: more waves per second results in a higher note (higher frequency); fewer waves per second results in a lower note (lower frequency). Now ask:

- Which notes result from more waves per second (shorter wavelength), and which notes result from fewer waves per second (longer wavelength)?

- Do you have any predictions about how the wavelengths of the two octave notes are related?

In a musical scale, features such as major thirds and fourths (and many others) also have strict mathematical relationships that you may want to explore with your child.

These can be explored by experimenting with the Harmonics activity in the Chrome Music Lab (musiclab.chromeexperiments.com/Harmonics). Students with a sharp ear will be able to hear the similarity in pitch between the strings with these numerical relationships. For example, listen for the similarities between the strings with one, two, and four nodes.

"Mathematical Harmonies"

Petersen explains the phenomenon in this way: "If we could watch our simple string vibrate with a slow motion camera, we would see that it vibrates in many modes … The main mode is the fundamental frequency or first harmonic, and gives the note its specified frequency."

Scan the QR code to read Petersen's paper in full and to get more details on the harmonics of a vibrating string.

For advanced learners, explore the mathematics of many octaves. Graph the curve showing the frequencies of five octaves. For example, for note "A," start at 110 and graph the points:

- 1110
- 2220
- 3440
- 4880
- 51760

This is an exponential curve.

For very advanced learners, explore how the decibel scale works mathematically. Remember, a decibel is a unit of measure for the loudness of a sound, which is also the amplitude of the vibration making that sound. The decibel scale is logarithmic. As an example, a sound that measures 30 decibels is **ten times** louder than a sound that measures 20 decibels. And 40 decibels is ten times louder than 30 decibels. Advanced students might graph this logarithmic curve.

Engineering: Communications Engineering

A cup-and-string telephone is an easy, fun experiment that goes way back—grandparents and even great-grandparents may have done this activity when they were children. This activity reinforces the idea that sound creates vibrations and vibrations create sound. It also allows children to test different solutions to the same problem in an iterative fashion.

NGSS Engineering Design Standards

The engineering design challenge in this chapter provides opportunities for children to develop understanding of the NGSS Engineering Design Standards identified here.

K-2 ACTIVITIES	3-5 ACTIVITIES
K-2-ETS1-3. Analyze data from tests of two objects designed to solve the same problem to compare the strengths and weaknesses of how each performs.	**3-5-ETS1-2.** Generate and compare multiple possible solutions to a problem based on how well each is likely to meet the criteria and constraints of the problem.

Getting Started

Help your children make a cup-and-string telephone (Figure 7.3). Punch a small hole in the bottom of each of the two cups. Feed the string through the hole from the outside in, and either tie a fat knot that won't slip out, or use a paperclip, toothpick, washer, etc. to tie to the string so it won't slip out of the hole when the string is pulled tight. Attach the string to both cups in this fashion.

Grade-Level Guidelines

Here are grade-appropriate experiments to explore more aspects of sound.

Grades K–2

Have two children (or you and your child) each take a cup and walk away from each other until the string pulls taut (not so tight that the cups tear!). Have one person hold the cup to their ear, and have the other person talk quietly. Then reverse. Can each person be heard by the other?

Ask the children: "Now that you know how sound works, please explain how the cup-and-string telephone works."

Now, while the two participants are using the cup-and-string phone, have someone else pinch the string somewhere along the way. What happens? Next, have the participants try to use the phone with the string drooping rather than taut. What happens? Why?

Finally, create two columns on a chalkboard or whiteboard. Label one "Cup-and-string" and the other "Cell phone." Under each column write good and bad characteristics of each method of communication. Put a plus next to good characteristics and a minus next to bad characteristics. How do the two forms of communication compare?

Figure 7.3 You can try many experiments with a simple cup-and-string telephone.

Grades 3–5

Create a cup-and-string telephone as described above, using string and the smallest-sized cups for your first test. Take turns talking and listening. Note the sound quality. Now replace the string with fishing line and repeat the test. Finally replace the string with yarn. Take notes on the sound quality of each.

Carry out the same experiment with the next larger size cups and each type of string, one by one. Again, take notes on each.

Now use the largest size cups and each type of string, one by one. Take notes on each.

Did you find a certain combination of cup and string gave you a better, clearer, or louder experience? If so, why do you think there was improvement with that combination?

Do you think coffee cans might provide good sound quality? Why or why not?

Extensions and Connections

Children's Literature. Children's books are an excellent way for kids to learn more about sound waves and how sound works. Possible titles for this project include: *Let's Ride a Wave!* by Chris Ferrie, *How Sound Moves* by Sharon Coan, and *Clang!* by Darcy Pattison. *What Are Sound Waves* by Robin Johnson includes the opportunity for children to demonstrate knowledge by creating their own sound devices.

Fine Arts. Grade K–2 students could draw a picture of the experiment showing dry rice vibrating from a nearby sound source. They should label their drawing with everything that's vibrating to create this effect, and then explain carefully to a friend or family member how and why the experiment works. Grade K–5 children could draw a picture of the cup-and-string phone, label the drawing to show how the device works, and then carefully explain to a friend or family member how and why the experiment works.

Life Science. See the amazing sight of a frog's song causing vibrations in the puddle he's sitting in. You can "see" the sound waves! If they can't find their own frog to observe, children could watch the video at bit.ly/2KZ0aJJ.

It's a Zoo in Here!

This series of activities draws upon children's interests in animals to explore STEM content and make cross-curricular connections. The overarching challenge for this project is for children to design a zoo. The format and level of sophistication for the zoo will depend on grade level; an individual child's assets, needs, and interests; materials available; and time spent on the activity. The entire project could be adapted to reflect children's individual interests or local context. For instance, if a child is especially interested in marine animals, all activities could focus on designing an aquarium rather than a zoo. And virtual field trips or animal choices could draw upon local zoo resources and ecosystems with which the child is familiar. Teachers, families, and children should tailor this STEM project to best meet individual needs and interests.

ISTE Standards for Students

You can use technology resources to get children interested in the project, develop some background knowledge, or extend math and science activities. The activities throughout this chapter align best with the following ISTE Standards for Students. Additional connections with ISTE Standards can occur when students use multimedia resources to present and share their work with others.

Empowered Learner

1c. Students use technology to seek feedback that informs and improves their practice and to demonstrate their learning in a variety of ways.

Knowledge Constructor

3a. Students plan and employ effective research strategies to locate information and other resources for their intellectual or creative pursuits.

3c. Students curate information from digital resources using a variety of tools and methods to create collections of artifacts that demonstrate meaningful connections or conclusions.

3d. Students build knowledge by actively exploring real-world issues and problems, developing ideas and theories and pursuing answers and solutions.

Innovative Designer

4b. Students select and use digital tools to plan and manage a design process that considers design constraints and calculated risks.

4d. Students exhibit a tolerance for ambiguity, perseverance and the capacity to work with open-ended problems.

Computational Thinker

5c. Students break problems into component parts, extract key information, and develop descriptive models to understand complex systems or facilitate problem-solving.

Materials, Time, and Supervision

This project can draw from a variety of resources. Table 8.1 summarizes materials that are required and optional for activities in this chapter.

TABLE 8.1 Project Materials

REQUIRED	OPTIONAL
• Connected device (laptop, desktop, tablet, or smartphone)	• Video games and consoles
• Writing utensil (pen or pencil)	• Printouts of animal images
• Paper	• Small toy animal figurines
• Arts & crafts supplies (cardboard, glue, tape, string, markers)	• Blocks (wooden or LEGO)
• Ruler or tape measure	

It is expected that most children would spend a total of 10–20 hours on the activities in this project or between 2–3 hours a day for a week or two. Activity choices can be tailored to the available time commitment. While much of the project is designed for relatively independent work, questions and discussion prompts are provided throughout. Some children, especially early readers, will need oral directions to get started with the activities you select.

Resources to Explore and Inspire

Children can take virtual field trips of zoos and aquariums around the world or observe animals live via zoo webcams. A prior visit to a zoo is another rich source of conversation about zoo animals and habitats that could spark children's interest in this project, as are books and movies about zoos. Table 8.2 summarizes some technology resources to support children's exploration of topics in this chapter; additional suggestions are offered with the science and math activities.

TABLE 8.2 Resources to Explore: It's a Zoo in Here

RESOURCE	DESCRIPTION	GRADE LEVEL	CODE
PBS Zoo Field Trip	Virtual field trip to a zoo.	K–3	qrgo.page.link/J1Xij
San Diego Zoo	Videos and live cameras of animals at the San Diego Zoo.	K–5	qrgo.page.link/DhDVS
Georgia Aquarium	Live webcam of a beluga whale.	K–5	qrgo.page.link/W14nc
Houston Zoo	Live webcams of animals at the Houston Zoo.	K–5	qrgo.page.link/UnUvB
Monterey Bay Aquarium	Easily searchable information about over 200 aquatic animals.	K–5	qrgo.page.link/2x9Uy

(Continued)

RESOURCE	DESCRIPTION	GRADE LEVEL	CODE
Lincoln Children's Zoo	Video and 3D panoramas of cheetah habitats.	K–5	qrgo.page.link/9uccR
Smithsonian National Zoo	Live webcams of animals at the U.S. National Zoo.	K–5	qrgo.page.link/Zd9Ty
National Aquarium	Virtual tour of the U.S. National Aquarium.	K–5	qrgo.page.link/PuUL1
Zoology for Kids	Collection of resources and activities about zoos and animals.	K–5	qrgo.page.link/XuJqt
Association of Zoos & Aquariums	Educational resources about zoos, aquariums, and conservation.	K–5	qrgo.page.link/PGCYe

Science: Choosing and Researching Animals

After drawing children's interest in the topic of zoos, you can use that context to explore math and science content. Let children know they are going to design their own zoo, but first they have to learn about the animals that would be in their zoo, along with their habitats and needs. This activity can be adjusted for individual children based on age, interest, reading level, available resources, and prior knowledge.

NGSS Disciplinary Core Ideas for Science

Science learning activities in this chapter align with standards focused on observing and describing patterns of animal needs and behaviors in early grades. In later grades, standards emphasize constructing arguments and developing models to describe animal behaviors, habitats, and relationships.

K–2 ACTIVITIES	3–5 ACTIVITIES
K-LS1-1. Use observations to describe patterns of what plants and animals (including humans) need to survive.	**3-LS2-1.** Construct an argument that some animals form groups that help members survive.
1-LS1-2. Read texts and use media to determine patterns in behavior of parents and offspring that help offspring survive.	**3-LS4-3.** Construct an argument with evidence that in a particular habitat some organisms can survive well, some survive less well, and some cannot survive at all.
2-LS4-1. Make observations of plants and animals to compare the diversity of life in different habitats.	**5-LS2-1.** Develop a model to describe the movement of matter among plants, animals, decomposers, and the environment.

Getting Started

Choose animals for your zoo. Use books and online resources (approved websites or apps) to research zoo animals and their needs. Younger kids might choose two or three animals, while older students might investigate five or more animals. Use online research tools or library ebooks and resources to explore questions such as:

- What is the animal's species?

- How much space does each animal need?

- What kind of habitat does each animal need? What climate is appropriate for each animal?

- Do the animals need to be alone, in pairs, or in groups?

- What kind of safety barriers does each animal need to be in a zoo?

- What is the animal's diet?

- What is the animal's lifespan?

Animal research can be done in an open-ended fashion, or in a more structured way such as in Table 8.3. Adults or children could create a table such as this using a spreadsheet or word processing software to organize children's online research. Using a structure such as Table 8.3 may also help children notice similarities and differences across animals.

TABLE 8.3 Choosing Animals for Your Zoo

	ANIMAL 1	ANIMAL 2	ANIMAL 3	ANIMAL 4
What is the name of your animal?				
What is the animal's natural habitat?				
What is the climate where the animal lives in nature?				
Does the animal usually live alone, in pairs, or in groups? Why?				
Where does the animal get its energy? What is the animal's natural diet?				
Describe how the animal is born and raised. How long does the animal usually live in nature?				
What kind of barriers does the animal need to be in a zoo safely?				

Grade-Level Guidelines

Questions and discussions can be adapted to meet the grade levels and needs of individual children, and should align with grade-level science standards. Aligned sample questions and discussion topics are listed with each grade level below. Children should refer to their online research and use evidence to support their answers and discussion. Discussions can take place in online class discussion boards, during designated distance learning times, or more informally such as over dinner. Possible questions to prompt discussion are organized according to grade bands. While discussions should go beyond right or wrong answers, key ideas are included to help adults guide discussion. Adults could also use online searches to learn more about science ideas in advance of discussions.

Grades K–2

Children in early grades should develop an understanding of what animals need to survive and how they interact with their habitats. Online research will likely include investigation of these ideas, but the following questions and examples of some possible answers further reinforce these science concepts and encourage children to think across multiple animals.

- What does each animal need to survive?
  - Food
  - Water
  - Safety
- How are the animals' needs the same? How are they different?
  - All animals need water.
  - Some animals eat plants while others need meat as part of their diet.
- Why do you think the animal lives in their habitat? What does that habitat have that the animal needs? Can you draw a picture?
  - Animals who eat plants live in areas with the food they need.
  - Animals, plants, and surroundings make up a system or an ecosystem.
- Can you find out how the animal parents take care of their babies? How do the parents know what the babies need?

- Offspring make sounds or signals to communicate their needs.

- Parents respond by feeding, comforting, or protecting.

- Do some of your animals live in the same types of habitats? What other animals and animals live in those habitats?

  - Emphasize the diversity of living things in different habitats.

  - Different habitats support different ecosystems.

Grades 3–5

Older children may enjoy discussing the questions intended for younger children, but to address science standards for grades 3–5, these discussions should extend to include more about relationships between animals and their environment. The questions and ideas below can help adults prompt and guide meaningful science discussions with children in intermediate grades.

- Why do you think [selected animal] live in groups?

  - Survival

  - Obtaining food

  - Protection from environment or predators

  - Adapting to changes

- Do you think all of the animals you selected could live in a zoo in our town? Why or why not? (Emphasize the need to support their argument with evidence.)

  - Organisms and their habitats make up a system in which they depend on each other.

  - The climate, plant life, etc. in your area may or may not meet the needs and characteristics of the animals the child selected.

- Can you draw a picture to show the relationship between soil, air, water, plants, food, and your animal? How are they related?

  - Explore the food web to understand how matter is transferred within the ecosystem.

  - Learn more about food webs and relationships among animals and habitats by scanning the following QR codes.

Cycles of Matter and
Energy Transfer

Interdependent Relationships
in Ecosystems

Math: Measuring Length, Perimeter, and Area

Getting Started

When adults think of measurement, we tend to think of measurement tools such as rulers and measurement units such as inches or meters. But the International Vocabulary of Metrology defines measurement as a "process of experimentally obtaining one or more quantity values that can reasonably be attributed to a quantity" (JCGM, 2008, p.16). Measurement is a process involving attributes, quantities, and comparisons. Because of the complex nature of measurement, the math activities in this chapter may not look like what some adults recognize as "measurement".

It is important that children eventually learn to measure using standard units and tools, but children must make sense of underlying measurement concepts first. Research-based learning trajectories for measurement articulate the order in which early measurement concepts are best learned (Gravemeijer, Bowers, & Stephan, 2003; Szilagyi, Clements, & Sarama, 2013). Before learning to measure inches with rulers, children must understand what a unit is, that units must be consistent, and that measuring length of an object requires iterating the same unit, end-to-end from the beginning to the end of the object. Zoo-themed math activities in this chapter help children develop measurement concepts in the order suggested by learning trajectories and math standards. While it may be tempting to jump ahead to measuring lengths with rulers and standard units, a more patient approach can give kids a chance to develop deep understanding that will help them measure accurately and efficiently when they are ready.

CCSSM Math Content Stndards

To learn about mathematics in te context of designing a zoo, children can incorporate measurement topics across grade levels. Younger children can focus on direct comparison, while older children extend these ideas to explore measurement of length, perimeter, and area. Math activities in this chapter support the elementary math standards shown here.

K–2 ACTIVITIES	3–5 ACTIVITIES
CCSS.MATH.CONTENT.K.MD.A.2. Directly compare two objects with a measurable attribute in common, to see which object has "more of"/"less of" the attribute, and describe the difference.	**CCSS.MATH.CONTENT.3.MD.D.8.** Solve real world and mathematical problems involving perimeters of polygons, including finding the perimeter given the side lengths, finding an unknown side length, and exhibiting rectangles with the same perimeter and different areas or with the same area and different perimeters.
CCSS.MATH.CONTENT.1.MD.A.2. Express the length of an object as a whole number of length units, by laying multiple copies of a shorter object (the length unit) end to end; understand that the length measurement of an object is the number of same-size length units that span it with no gaps or overlaps.	**CCSS.MATH.CONTENT.4.MD.A.3.** Apply the area and perimeter formulas for rectangles in real world and mathematical problems.
CCSS.MATH.CONTENT.2.MD.A.4. Measure to determine how much longer one object is than another, expressing the length difference in terms of a standard length unit.	**CCSS.MATH.CONTENT.5.MD.A.1.** Convert among different-sized standard measurement units within a given measurement system (e.g., convert 5 cm to 0.05 m), and use these conversions in solving multi-step, real world problems.

Grade-Level Guidelines

Drawing from research-based learning trajectories about measurement, the math activities in this chapter are specified by grade level and grouped by grade band. Grade levels are determined by math standards, but individual children may be at a different place in the learning trajectory than their grade level would suggest. Educators can align zoo-themed math activities with the grade-level standards students are expected to master. The sequence of activities provided in this chapter should connect with measurement concepts in math curriculum, as well as offer ideas for supporting individual children who need additional support or enrichment

Grades K–2

Before children learn to measure, they should learn what attributes are measurable. Comparison helps build a good foundation for measuring. Some activities for kindergarteners might include providing images or cutouts of animals such as the ones in Figure 8.1. (Animal figurine toys would work well too!) Ask the child to choose two animals and pose questions that require the child to compare and reason about their measurable attributes (in real life).

- Which animal is taller?
- Which animal weighs less?
- Which animal is longer?

Figure 8.1 Young children can use images of animals or animal figures to compare sizes and attributes.

Zoo Animals—
Touch, Look, Listen

Alternatively, ask the child to draw two pictures: a monkey's zoo enclosure and an elephant's zoo enclosure. Discuss which enclosure is bigger. What does the child mean by bigger? "Bigger" might refer to the area of the enclosure or the length of the fence. Children could also use a zoo animal app to view animals and compare relative sizes of various animals. Scan the QR code for an example of an app for exploring zoo animals.

The focus in grade 1 is on understanding length measurement as end-to-end units of the same size. In later grades, they will learn to measure using standard units, such as inches or centimeters. Early measurers can use multiple animal cutout cards to measure household objects. For example, *How many panda cards long is the book? How many giraffe cards tall is the pitcher?* Figure 8.2 illustrates an example. It is important that children have two or more copies of the animal card with which they are measuring since that will be the unit they repeatedly lay end to end. Mixing up units (i.e., using a combination of multiple animal cards to measure the same object) would defeat the purpose of learning to measure at this stage. Of course, the animal cards are not drawn to scale, so emphasize the size of the cards, not the animals themselves.

Figure 8.2 Children can measure length of an object using animal cards as a unit.

Smithsonian's
National Zoo Small
Mammal House

Another alternative is to ask the child to stand against a wall and use a pencil to mark their height, as many families do to gauge growth over time. Choose a small zoo animal and look up the average height of that animal. Scan the QR code for information about small mammals at the Smithsonian National Zoo. Print or draw a picture of the animal on a realistic scale. Use two or more copies to measure how many small animals tall the child is. Figure 8.3 illustrates how a child could measure their height using a sand cat at the Smithsonian's National Zoo's Small Mammal House as the unit of measure.

Figure 8.3 Children can measure their height using a small zoo animal as the unit.

To expand the activity into the outdoors, ask the child to mark off the size of an enclosure for a small zoo animal (e.g., monkey or penguin). Ask the child to figure out how many "feet" of fencing the would need for the enclosure by carefully walking the perimeter, heel to toe. This activity could lay groundwork for later learning about perimeter. However, you will want to reinforce that their "feet" are likely not the same length as the standard 12-inch measure for feet.

In grade 2, children will begin to use standard units to measure. This could include activities such as asking a child to stand against a wall and use a pencil to mark their height, as many families do to gauge growth over time. Measure height to the nearest inch and compare with the typical height of the animals they selected for the science portion of their Measuring Length, Perimeter, and Area project. This is different from the activity in Figure 8.3 because children compare their height (in centimeters, inches, feet, or meters) to the height of an animal using the same measurement unit. In an outdoor space, children can mark off the size of an enclosure for each of two small zoo animals (e.g., monkey and penguin). Use a tape measure to measure, to the nearest foot, the length of fence needed for the enclosures and compare the lengths needed for the two animals.

Grades 3–5

Measurement activities for children in grades 3 through 5 shift from measuring length to measuring perimeter and area and comparing the two. To do this, ask the child to design one zoo enclosure for an animal of their choosing, following these steps:

1. Imagine you have 100 feet of fencing to make an enclosure for an animal. Use all 100 feet of fencing to design a rectangular enclosure with the largest area.

2. To figure out the largest possible enclosure, try drawing rectangles and show the length, width, perimeter (amount of fencing used), and area (room inside the enclosure).

3. Keep track of your work. (Organized lists or tables work well, but it can be more impactful to let children explore and figure this out versus telling them in the onset.)

4. Make a convincing argument for what rectangular enclosure has a perimeter of 100 feet and the largest area. How do you know the enclosure has the most area of any you could build with 100 feet of fencing?

This task aligns with measurement standards for grades 3–5 and engages students in open-ended problem-solving and reasoning. Students should find that the closer their rectangle gets to being a square, the larger the area. In doing so, they use ideas of addition, multiplication, perimeter, and area. Children may also demonstrate creativity by trying to place one side of the enclosure against a building so that fencing is only needed for three sides. This is a good example of contextualizing and decontextualizing to solve the problem, characteristic of the mathematical practice of reasoning abstractly and quantitatively, and does not fundamentally change the mathematical learning in the task.

A variety of technology tools can support exploration of length, area, and perimeter. Table 8.4 summarizes some options.

TABLE 8.4 Math Resources to Support It's a Zoo in Here

RESOURCE	DESCRIPTION	GRADE LEVEL	CODE
Math Learning Center Geoboard	Virtual geoboard and rubber bands for open-ended exploration and visualization of length, perimeter, and area.	K–5	qrgo.page.link/f9iW
PhET Area Builder	Interactive tool for building shapes and measuring the perimeter and area.	3–5	qrgo.page.link/mPFt
Toy Theater Area-Perimeter Explorer	Interactive tool for designing shapes with colorful blocks and exploring relationship between area and perimeter.	3–5	qrgo.page.link/J1tQi
Shodor Interactivate Shape Explorer	Interactive learning activity and connected resources for designing and measuring shapes on a grid.	3–5	qrgo.page.link/g2eqm

To extend the perimeter and area enclosure activity to address the grade 5 standard for comparing measurements within a given system, ask the child to convert the number of feet to yards or inches. To provide a more realistic context, suppose that fencing is sold in 20-meter rolls and they must determine how many rolls of fencing they will need for their enclosure. This task also requires students to contextualize and decontextualize. If fencing is sold in rolls, the student should realize that the rounding rules they are used to may not apply. In this case, if 61 meters of fencing is needed, three 20-meter rolls wouldn't be enough so the student would need to round up to 4 rolls.

Engineering: Civil Engineering

Types of Engineering
for Kids' Exploration

Designing a zoo is an example of the type of work civil engineers might do. Children can learn more about civil engineering careers by scanning the QR code.

After developing an understanding of zoos through technology, science, and mathematics, it's time to design and build a zoo! This is a space and time for the child to be creative and adapt the project to their own interests and talents. Younger children can sketch a zoo design for the animals they selected during the science exploration. To maintain a focus on engineering, remind the child of the problem at hand: design a zoo that meets the animal's needs and is safe for humans to visit. Also encourage children to make plans and prototypes before jumping ahead to their final designs; this is an important component of the engineering design process.

The specificity of design details can be adapted for each child. Engage children to think about how the shape of their zoo enclosures meet the animals' needs and what it would be like for humans to visit their zoo. Pose questions such as:

- Is there a sidewalk for zoo visitors that goes in front of all enclosures?
- Is it accessible to visitors who have disabilities?
- Are the enclosures big enough to meet the animals' needs?
- How will animals be protected during extreme weather?

After sketching their zoo and considering how it functions to solve the given problem, the child can build a model of their zoo using a variety of materials.

Blocks (wooden, interlocking bricks, etc.), household objects, and craft items such as cardboard boxes, toilet paper rolls, yarn, glue, craft sticks, and pipe cleaners can be creatively combined to construct a physical model of the child's zoo.

Older children can also sketch a zoo design, but you may provide more specificity and constraints. A more age-appropriate problem might be to design a zoo that meets the animals' needs, is safe for humans to visit, and can be contained within a 50-acre plot of land. Better yet, ask the child to choose constraints for the zoo they will be designing and help them determine whether those constraints are reasonable.

ZAA Accreditation

Discuss with the child some criteria for a successful zoo design. Of course, the design will contain nowhere near the level of detail and sophistication that actual zoos must consider, but you can draw upon habitat standards defined by the Zoological Association of America (scan the QR code to view the guidelines).

Some basic questions to consider for children's zoo designs might include:

- Does each animal have enough space to live safely and comfortably in their enclosure?

- Will the enclosures be tall enough to keep humans and animals safe?

- Is there an appropriate number of each type of animal? Some animals function better alone while others should be in pairs or groups. This information should be available from their science exploration.

- Does each animal have appropriate shelter, especially during extreme weather?

- Do the enclosures include features of the animals' native habitats?

- Can people with different types of disabilities access all of the zoo exhibits?

Older children can also turn their sketches into physical models. Blocks (wooden, LEGO, etc.), household objects, and craft items such as cardboard boxes, toilet paper rolls, yarn, glue, craft sticks, and pipe cleaners can be creatively combined to construct a physical model of the child's zoo. One might reasonably expect older children to use more precise measurements and even some rough scaling of their model, though more sophisticated scale drawings are not included in math standards until grade 7.

NGSS Engineering Design Standards

The engineering design challenge in this chapter provides opportunities for children to develop understanding of the NGSS Engineering Design Standards identified here.

K-2 ACTIVITIES	3-5 ACTIVITIES
K-2-ETS1-2. Develop a simple sketch, drawing, or physical model to illustrate how the shape of an object helps it function as needed to solve a given problem.	**3-5-ETS1-1.** Define a simple design problem reflecting a need or a want that includes specified criteria for success and constraints on materials, time, or cost.

Extensions and Connections

Entertainment. Children can continue to learn about zoos and animals through games and movies. Several video games focus on designing and running zoos, often with sophisticated levels of detail that could significantly extend children's learning. Some online games include *My Free Zoo, Planet Zoo,* and *Switch Zoo.* Other games are available for a variety of platforms including *Zoo Tycoon* (PC, Xbox, Steam games, Nintendo Switch) and *FUN! FUN! Animal Park* (Nintendo Switch). Younger children can explore online games such as *Wild Kratts* options at PBS Kids online. Movies and television shows can also extend and bridge between learning and entertainment. Movie options rated G or PG include: *We Bought a Zoo, Madagascar, The Wild, Free Willy,* and *Zootopia.* Television shows could include *The Wild Thornberries, Wild Kratts, The Crocodile Hunter,* or a variety of shows on the Animal Planet cable network. Of course, educators and families will select appropriate animal- and zoo-themed entertainment connections based on children's age, media availability, screen-time considerations, and adult judgment.

Children's Literature. Children's books about animals and zoos abound. Very young children might enjoy books such as *Good Night, Gorilla* by Peggy Rathmann, *Dear Zoo* by Rod Campbell, or Eric Carle's *1, 2, 3 to the Zoo.* Other zoo-themed titles include Dr. Seuss's *If I Ran the Zoo, The One and Only Ivan* by Katherine Applegate, and *Curious George* books from Margret and H. A. Rey. A full list of children's books that could connect with zoos is beyond the scope of this book. Books of children's choice about animals, zoos, or habitats can suitably support the STEM activities focused on designing a zoo.

Writing. A number of writing prompts could accompany this project. Children could be asked to tell a story about a day at their zoo. Consider doing so from the perspective of not just a visitor, but from the perspective of a zookeeper or even an animal. Younger children can and should draw pictures to accompany their writing. Children in later grades might also engage in writing that considers the ethics of zoos, whether in general or for specific animals. For instance, some would argue that elephants should never be kept in zoos. Ask the child to research the topic using age-appropriate, accurate, credible sources and to write a brief essay (or presentation) that communicates a well-supported point of view about the issue.

Social Studies. Ask children to identify their animals' natural habitats on a map. You could also ask them to locate virtual field trip sites on a map. Some options include looking at maps together and pointing out locations, printing out coloring sheets of maps from sites such as supercoloring.com, or using an online coloring site such as thecolor.com to explore maps.

Fine arts. Art can be incorporated in the design of zoo drawings and in the math enclosure activity. Other possible connections include viewing online artwork created by animals (e.g., search online for the New Mexico Biopark Society's animal art or the Saint Louis Zoo's animal artwork) and trying to recreate the same style of paintings. Doing so could help children focus on the scientific ideas of structure and function in various animals and how they create the pieces of art.

Computer Science. Computer science can be incorporated in age-appropriate ways during the design of children's zoos. Students could recreate or import images of sketches into block programming environments, such as Scratch, and write creative puzzle-piece programs for animals and people in the zoos. Alternatively, if children have access to educational robotics, they could program a Dash or Sphero robot to take someone on a tour of their zoo. A child with access to an Ozobot robot could draw paths within their zoos for the robot to follow, as though it were a visitor. Also be sure to check the website for your robot; many offer online curriculum and projects that may be zoo-themed. Online tools such as Tinkercad and Google SketchUp could also be used to render models of students' zoo designs.

Going Viral

The COVID-19 pandemic illuminates the importance of STEM literacy for the general public and how multiple areas of STEM expertise must converge to find solutions to serious societal challenges. Since the pandemic serves as such a powerful example of the need for integrated STEM approaches, this last project focuses on science, technology, engineering, and math concepts related to epidemiology. Educators and families can incorporate this project into distance learning to help children better understand STEM concepts behind how diseases spread and how to prevent or control them. Although efforts have been made to approach these topics gently, adults should exercise caution if incorporating this project into distance learning for children who have recently suffered negative impacts of contagious disease in their household, family, or community. For some children, knowledge can provide comfort and a way to cope with complex topics, but for other children, it may exacerbate trauma. As with all projects in this book, educators and families are encouraged to select, adapt, and enrich the connected activities in this project to best meet the needs of individual children.

. . . .

ISTE Standards for Students

Using technology to explore and support learning about infectious diseases can deepen math and science learning and aligns with the ISTE Standards for Students. Interactive games allow students to explore content in ways that offer student choices and instant feedback. Communicating their ideas to peers and adults through a variety of digital means also deepens student learning with technology. The ISTE Standards that most align with activities in this chapter are shown below.

Empowered Learner

1c. Students use technology to seek feedback that informs and improves their practice and to demonstrate their learning in a variety of ways.

Knowledge Constructor

3d. Students build knowledge by actively exploring real-world issues and problems, developing ideas and theories and pursuing answers and solutions.

Innovative Designer

4a. Students know and use a deliberate design process for generating ideas, testing theories, creating innovative artifacts or solving authentic problems.

4d. Students exhibit a tolerance for ambiguity, perseverance and the capacity to work with open-ended problems.

Computational Thinker

5c. Students break problems into component parts, extract key information, and develop descriptive models to understand complex systems or facilitate problem-solving.

Creative Communicator

6c. Students communicate complex ideas clearly and effectively by creating or using a variety of digital objects such as visualizations, models, or simulations.

. . . .

Materials, Time, and Supervision

Table 9.1 includes the materials needed for activities in this chapter. Because the engineering design challenge is open to students' choices and ideas, the materials will vary. Remind children that designing within the constraints of available materials is a realistic aspect of engineering.

TABLE 9.1 Project Materials

REQUIRED	OPTIONAL
• Connected device (laptop, desktop, tablet, or smartphone) • Writing utensil (pen or pencil) • Paper • Art supplies (markers, colored pencils)	• Soap • Plate or shallow bowl • Glitter or pepper • 4 slices of bread • 4 reusable zipper-locking bags • Any materials desired for the open-ended design challenge

Project activities in this chapter can be embedded within an online learning management system or completed independently at home to supplement formal distance instruction. Overall, the project can be completed in about a week, but could be spaced out or enriched to last closer to two weeks. Many children can complete the online games and most activities in this project independently, but younger children may need additional guidance or reading support. Adult supervision and input will be needed as children embark on the most open-ended engineering project in this book.

Resources to Explore and Inspire

You can use technology to introduce children to some of the basic aspects of infectious diseases or as a follow-up to more hands-on science and math activities. This could include accessing curated material online. Given the possibility for internet searches that provide alarming results for young children, adults should definitely monitor and provide guidance when children seek online information about disease transmission and causes. With adult guidance, children could look up information about the common cold, such as how it is spread, prevented, and treated. You may want to avoid examples that yield graphic, potentially disturbing images.

Children should also be prompted to explore and discuss how diseases spread, how they are prevented, and how they are treated. Obviously, the level of detail should be tailored to the age and maturity level of the child. Kids of all ages can understand that many diseases can be spread through the air or touching surfaces; the importance of handwashing, masks, and hygiene for preventing disease spread; that some diseases can be prevented through vaccines; that diseases vary in their severity; and that some diseases are curable with medication, while others can only be treated for symptoms. Adults may also discuss the various medical technologies that children have observed in their own experiences (e.g., thermometers and blood pressure cuffs).

Table 9.2 summarizes some technology resources to support children's exploration of topics in this chapter. Many of the games and resources in this table offer interactive explorations that embed math and science content related to epidemiology, disease spread, and public health.

TABLE 9.2 Resources to Explore: Going Viral

RESOURCE	DESCRIPTION	GRADE LEVEL	CODE
World of Viruses	Online collection of comics, apps, and resources about viruses and microbes.	K–5	qrgo.page.link/NwWzZ
Cambridge Infectious Diseases	Collection of online games about disease, pandemics, and medical research.	3–5	qrgo.page.link/f1JLN
U.S. Centers for Disease Control and Prevention	Solve the Outbreak, an interactive game, engages children in epidemiological challenges to interpret hints and clues, analyze data, and fight disease outbreaks.	3–5	qrgo.page.link/pYe3d

Science: Infection Inventor

Interactive games in Table 9.2 emphasize the patterns in disease spread and the cause and effect of diseases. To delve deeper into these ideas, children apply their knowledge in a creative way and conduct experiments about infectious disease and hygiene. Unlike prior chapters that divided science activities into K–2 and 3–5 grade bands, this chapter highlights activities that are accessible and appropriate for children across grades K–5.

Health and medical science are not explicitly included in elementary science standards, because they typically fall under the purview of health classes in elementary grades. However, these topics are important in a scientifically literate society and health careers draw upon a great deal of science. In this chapter, some science emphasis can be placed on understanding that diseases are caused by germs (bacteria and viruses) that are too small to see.

NGSS Disciplinary Core Ideas for Science

Whereas Chapters 2 through 8 align science activities with Disciplinary Core Ideas for grade bands K–2 and 3–5, Going Viral science activities are aligned with NGSS Crosscutting Concepts that span science content all grade levels.

NGSS CROSSCUTTING CONCEPTS

Patterns. Observed patterns in nature guide organization and classification and prompt questions about relationships and causes underlying them.

Cause and Effect. Events have causes, sometimes simple, sometimes multifaceted. Deciphering causal relationships and the mechanisms by which they are mediated is a major activity of science and engineering.

Getting Started

The main science activity in this project asks children to invent their own disease. Children can determine a name for their disease and consider what causes it, how it spreads, what the symptoms are, and how it is treated. Creativity and some silliness are welcome, but the activity should prompt children to think and apply ideas about disease cause, prevention, spread, and treatment. Kids can also create drawings of what their virus or bacteria looks like under a microscope. Figure 9.1 is an example of what the activity might look like.

Name of Disease: *Ear Flu*

Draw a picture of what the germ looks like under a microscope.

What causes the disease?
Earmonster germs.

How is the disease transmitted?
From touching earwax.

Do many people get the disease? Why?
No because you don't usually touch earwax, especially other people's.

What are its symptoms?
Headaches, fever, and earaches.

How can the disease be prevented?
By not touching people's ears and washing your hands if you do.

How is the disease treated? Can it be cured?
Drops of medicine in the ear and fever medicine make it feel better, but it can't be cured.

Figure 9.1 Children apply science content knowledge and creativity to invent a disease.

Grade-Level Guidelines

Inventing their own disease and its characteristics prompts children to consider important aspects of diseases. Further discussion is needed to unpack the NGSS Crosscutting Concepts about patterns and cause–effect relationships. Using an online discussion board, multimedia presentation, or informal conversation, ask children to explain what an outbreak of their disease might be like. They should consider what patterns might indicate an outbreak, what could cause the outbreak, and what effect it would have on individuals and the public. These conversations can extend the Infection Inventor from a fun activity that involves science into relevant, authentic consideration of scientific concepts.

In addition to the Infection Inventor activity and discussion, children can engage in common hands-on experiments to explore the science of handwashing. Here are two experiments that children can do using common household materials. Both experiments are appropriate for children in grades K–5; additional guidance and supervision is recommended for younger learners.

Soap Experiment

This experiment illustrates how handwashing with soap can repel germs (represented by pepper flakes or glitter).

1. Wash hands, and choose a clean workspace for the experiment.

2. Fill a clean plate or shallow bowl with water.

3. Generously sprinkle glitter or pepper flakes on top of the water.

4. Place a finger in the water. The child should notice that it becomes covered in pepper or glitter.

5. Coat another finger with soap. Place it in the water. The child should notice that the pepper or glitter moves away from the soap.

6. Wash hands to remove pepper, glitter, and/or soap.

Questions for the child to consider and discuss:

• What did you notice in this experiment?

• What is different between the two fingers you put in the water?

• What does the pepper/glitter represent?

• What does this experiment teach you about handwashing?

Bread Experiment

This experiment shows differences between germs on clean versus dirty hands.

1. Choose a clean workspace for the experiment.

2. Choose four slices of bread and place them on a clean plate or surface. Have four zippered plastic bags ready near the bread slices.

3. Use tongs or a fork to carefully place one slice of bread in a bag. Seal the bag and label it "Control."

4. Pick up a slice of bread and rub it on a high-use dirty surface such as a phone, remote control, or computer keyboard. Place the bread in a bag. Seal the bag, and label it with the type of surface the bread touched.

5. Pick up a slice of bread and pat both sides with your unwashed hands. Place the bread in a bag. Seal the bag, and label it "unwashed hands."

6. Wash hands with soap and water, and dry thoroughly. Pick up the fourth slice of bread and pat both sides with your clean hands. Place the bread in a bag. Seal the bag, and label it "clean hands."

7. Place all four bags of bread in a dark, dry, cool place and observe daily to see changes. A daily photo journal would work great for this! Mold should begin growing on some of the bread slices.

8. After about a week, discuss the differences between the four slices of bread. Theoretically, the amount of mold should range from least to most in this order: control, clean hands, unwashed hands, dirty surface.

Questions for the child to consider and discuss:

- What did you notice in this experiment?

- What do you think caused more mold to grow on some pieces of bread than others?

- What is the relationship between what the bread touched and the amount of mold?

Math: How Sickness Spreads

Diseases spread exponentially, a mathematical relationship that is not always well understood in society at large. Exponents do not appear in Common Core math standards until the middle grades and exponential growth is typically in high school math curriculum. But elementary children can develop understanding of numbers, operations, and algebraic relationships that will help them better understand exponential growth patterns in later grades. The types of math problems identified in this chapter can be adapted from regular math curriculum to include the context of disease spread, or new tasks can be created that extend the Infection Inventor activity.

CCSSM Math Content Stndards

Going Viral math activities focus on Operations and Algebraic Thinking standards. These standards involve solving word problems with addition, subtraction, multiplication, and division, as well as identifying and generating numerical patterns.

K-2 ACTIVITIES	3-5 ACTIVITIES
CCSS.MATH.CONTENT.K.OA.A.1. Represent addition and subtraction with objects, fingers, mental images, drawings, sounds (e.g., claps), acting out situations, verbal explanations, expressions, or equations.	**CCSS.MATH.CONTENT.3.OA.D.9.** Identify arithmetic patterns (including patterns in the addition table or multiplication table), and explain them using properties of operations.
CCSS.MATH.CONTENT.1.OA.A.2. Solve word problems that call for addition of three whole numbers whose sum is less than or equal to 20, e.g., by using objects, drawings, and equations with a symbol for the unknown number to represent the problem.	**CCSS.MATH.CONTENT.4.OA.A.2.** Multiply or divide to solve word problems involving multiplicative comparison, e.g., by using drawings and equations with a symbol for the unknown number to represent the problem, distinguishing multiplicative comparison from additive comparison.
CCSS.MATH.CONTENT.2.OA.A. Use addition and subtraction within 100 to solve one- and two-step word problems involving situations of adding to, taking from, putting together, taking apart, and comparing, with unknowns in all positions, e.g., by using drawings and equations with a symbol for the unknown number to represent the problem.	**CCSS.MATH.CONTENT.4.OA.C.5.** Generate a number or shape pattern that follows a given rule. Identify apparent features of the pattern that were not explicit in the rule itself.

Getting Started

Children can solve a variety of word problems related to the Going Viral context. But how children solve these problems may look different from how some adults would approach them. Children may draw pictures, count with their fingers, or write equations to make sense of word problems. And the equations may even look different from what you would write. Word problems can have different structures such as joining, separating, part-part-whole, or comparison. On top of that, problems may ask children to figure out a result, a change, or a starting quantity (Carpenter, Fennema, & Franke, 1996).

It's not necessary to explicitly teach about each type of word problem structure, but it is important to recognize that different structures invite different representations, strategies, and equations. What you may read and immediately interpret as $11 - 2 = $ __, a child might interpret as __ $+ 2 = 11$. The end result is the same, but give children the chance to solve problems in ways that make sense to them before stepping in too soon. Many teachers and curricula introduce strategies to help children make sense of different word problem structures. Sometimes these strategies may look unfamiliar or inefficient to families, but they can be an important bridge toward accurately and efficiently solving mathematical word problems.

Keyword strategies are often used for solving word problems. However, research suggests that keyword strategies are ineffective and can cause more harm than help (Karp, Bush, & Dougherty, 2019). Associating words like "in all" with addition or "left" with subtraction often glosses over what a word problem is asking and leads children to rush to incorrect solutions. Using a keyword strategy may lead children to underline two numbers in the problem and the words "in all" and then automatically add the two numbers together. However, if the problem is a "start unknown" problem, adding the two numbers together will not yield the correct answer since the total is already included in the problem. Similarly, underlining numbers and the word "left" in a word problem may lead children to write and solve a subtraction equation. But, what if the problem asks for the total number of flowers in someone's right and left hands? Dual meaning of the word "left" can lead to overgeneralizing keywords. Instead of relying on keyword strategies, encourage children to solve Going Viral math problems by reading and understanding the problem, considering the information that is given and what is unknown, choosing a strategy to solve the problem, and using what they know to find a solution.

Recommendations for getting started with Going Viral word problems apply across grades K–5, but activities in later grades focus more on patterns. Again, encourage children to think carefully about problems and draw from the strategies and representations that make sense to them. Representing patterns in tables or lists can be helpful, as can equations or verbal explanations. Supporting children's diverse ways of thinking and knowing encourages their problem-solving and positive dispositions toward mathematics.

Grade-Level Guidelines

Going Viral math activities support student understanding of operations and algebraic thinking in grades K–5. In early grades, children focus on strategies and representations for solving addition and subtraction word problems, all within the infectious disease context. During the grade 3–5 grade band, children continue to solve word problems, but also use multiplication and division. Across all elementary grades, children can identify and use mathematical patterns to solve problems. A focus on patterns connects well with the NGSS Crosscutting Concept of patterns and lends well to the context of how diseases spread among populations. Patterns in early grades tend to be arithmetic, or increasing by a constant amount (e.g., add three each time). Toward the end of elementary grades, children start exploring geometric patterns formed by multiplication or division. Exponential growth patterns are most relevant for disease spread, but are an extension within this chapter because exponential growth is not typically part of math curriculum for elementary grades.

Grades K–2

In earlier grades, children can create and solve problems about the spread of their invented disease. The youngest learners might use drawings to represent problems such as what happens if three people have Ear Flu and then three more people get infected. This could be expanded to also include three more people getting infected.

Vary the types and structures of word problems. The way children think about and solve "add to" problems is different from how they approach "comparison" problems. Consider the "add to" problem: 11 people have Ear Flu. Then more people get Ear Flu and now a total of 33 people have Ear Flu. How many additional people got Ear Flu? While adults might expect children to immediately write and solve the equation $33 - 11 = 22$, children may not approach the problem in that way. They might write an equation that more directly models the situation, $11 + \_\_ = 33$ and solve for the unknown addend (a group of numbers added together to form a sum). Many kids also rely on drawings or representations to solve problems. In this case, children might draw 11 marks and then draw more while counting up to 33 and then count the additional marks they made.

Contrast that with a problem such as: Rocktown has 42 cases of Ear Flu. Bernville has 86 cases. How many more cases does Bernville have than Rocktown? Most adults would still see $86 - 42 = 44$. To children, though, representing this problem with an equation or drawing may be more difficult. For a comparison problem such as this, a child might use a comparison bar, as shown in Figure 9.2. Notice that the bars do not need to be proportional, but the structure of the representation helps children organize the information in the word problem so they know to solve the problem $86 - 42 = 44$.

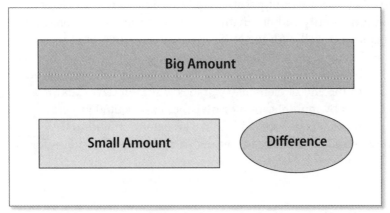

Figure 9.2 Children can use a comparison bar to organize information in word problems.

Grades 3–5

In later grades, students could explore algebraic relationships involving the spread of their fictitious disease. At first, children might consider an arithmetic pattern such as the Ear Flu growing by five new cases every day. Or they can look at a table of data showing a constant daily increase and figure out the pattern for themselves. To avoid misconceptions about disease transmission, pair this math activity with discussion about how diseases actually spread. Use a tree diagram that starts with five cases and assumes that each person infects one more person, as shown in Figure 9.3. Doing so should allow children to notice that disease transmission is not an arithmetic relationship, but instead can grow much faster. To help students discover the pattern, you might also test what happens if each person infects three or four people. For children to see how quickly exponential relationships can grow, explore what happens after five, six, or seven days of transmission. Children could also compare the number of cases if there is an arithmetic pattern as compared to an exponential pattern.

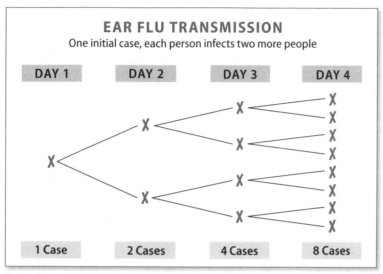

EAR FLU TRANSMISSION
One initial case, each person infects two more people

| DAY 1 | DAY 2 | DAY 3 | DAY 4 |

| 1 Case | 2 Cases | 4 Cases | 8 Cases |

Figure 9.3 A tree diagram illustrates exponential growth of Ear Flu.

Spread of Disease
Interactive

As an extension, educators and families could introduce technical terms associated with disease transmission such as R0 (pronounced "R naught"), the average number of new cases each case will transmit. Scan the QR code to find a mathematical simulation with more sophisticated explorations of how diseases spread when parameters such as initial number of cases and R0 vary.

Engineering: Biomedical Engineering

Types of Engineering
for Kids' Exploration

Some of the more obvious careers relating to infectious disease control and treatment are doctors, nurses, and epidemiologists. But children can also learn about how biomedical engineers help solve and prevent public health problems. To learn more about the STEM career field of biomedical engineering, scan the QR code. Many articles about how engineers have helped find solutions during the COVID-19 pandemic have been written and are just an internet search away (but keep in mind that you may wish to closely monitor children's searching, as there is also distressing information on this topic available online).

To encourage children to think like an engineer and utilize the engineering design process, try an open-ended challenge. All other projects in this book have defined a problem for which students design a solution. Instead, ask children to pose a problem relating to either their invented disease or a real disease, and then design a solution to help solve that problem. Of course, children will likely not develop a breakthrough vaccine at their kitchen table, but kids can use their creativity and household materials to engineer personal protective equipment (PPE) to protect from infection or tools to reduce contact with public surfaces and reduce transmission. For example, during the COVID-19 pandemic, people throughout the world invented new ways to make and sanitize facemasks and face shields. These design solutions involved tools ranging from a simple sock and scissors to 3D printers. In the example of Ear Flu, a child might explore a way to reduce exposure to earwax. A possible solution might be sealed containers for disposing cotton swabs (not recommended for insertion in the ear canal, but often used to clean exterior ear surfaces). They might use empty tubing and caps to create sealed containers the size of standard cotton swabs. In this project, children's problems and solutions will be constrained by the tools and resources they have at their disposal. This is consistent with engineering in the real world.

NGSS Engineering Design Standards

The engineering design challenge in this chapter provides opportunities for children to develop understanding of the NGSS Engineering Design Standards identified here.

K–2 ACTIVITIES	3–5 ACTIVITIES
K-2-ETS1-2. Develop a simple sketch, drawing, or physical model to illustrate how the shape of an object helps it function as needed to solve a given problem.	**3-5-ETS1-1.** Define a simple design problem reflecting a need or a want that includes specified criteria for success and constraints on materials, time, or cost

Extensions and Connections

Entertainment. Few movies, video games, or television programs that focus on disease transmissions are geared toward elementary children. A few programs such as episodes of PBS's *Daniel Tiger* focus on handwashing, illness, and hygiene, as do episodes of *Sesame Street*. For a sillier take on disease transmission, consider the *SpongeBob SquarePants* Season 1 episode "Suds." In terms of games, one thematic option is the board game *Pandemic*, which is geared toward children age 8 and older.

Children's Literature. Children can practice reading while learning more about germs and disease. Many fiction and nonfiction books include themes about disease or germs. Some possible fiction books on this topic include *Bubble* by Stewart Foster, *Dragons Get Colds Too* by Rebecca Roan, *Sick Simon* by Dan Krall, and *Cutie Sue Fights the Germs* by Kate Melton. *Love Without Hugs* by Jere Confrey explains the concept of disease carriers and social distancing while acknowledging children's emotions during a pandemic.

Writing. To incorporate writing into this project, children can write about their invented infections. Possible writing tasks include writing a news story about an outbreak of their disease or creating a comic strip about the how their disease is transmitted and eventually defeated.

Social Studies. Managing diseases as a matter of public health is a good opportunity for students to learn about communities. Infectious diseases can impact entire communities (as well as states, countries, or regions). Some communities may be hit harder than others—due to fewer resources and other factors. Children can learn about the resources and strategies communities use to keep people healthy.

Robotics. In child-friendly coding environments, children can model how diseases spread. Especially after learning about some mathematics involved in disease transmission, children could write programs to show how the disease they invented spreads.

Designing Distance Learning for Elementary STEM

The projects in this book offer a range of possibilities for thematic, project-based elementary STEM learning that can support distance learning. But why stop there? What if you have children who are captivated by dinosaurs? Or castles? Or soccer? With some creativity and consideration of STEM subject expectations, you can turn children's passions into educational projects of your own. This chapter walks you through the structure and thinking behind how this book's STEM projects are designed so you can extend the learning beyond the lessons in this book.

Extending Distance Learning

Here are the key steps for developing the types of projects presented in this book.

Choose a topic for your theme.

Start with what the child or children are passionate about. A child who loves mermaids could learn about STEM by leveraging that interest. For instance, the "It's a Zoo in Here" project in Chapter 8 could be adapted to that interest by focusing on animals that live in oceans. Be sure the topic is specific enough to connect with children's interests but also broad enough to include plenty of STEM connections and activities.

Identify science and math content connections you can make to that topic.

Maybe your theme suggests certain math and science connections, like the space project in this book. But think more specifically about the math and science content kids could *learn* in relation to your project theme, not just incidental connections. This is especially true with math where, too often, the presence of numbers or basic measurements are accepted as "math" within a STEM project. Ask yourself, What math are children actually learning? And how will they discuss, apply, and reflect on what they're learning about math in the project?

Keep in mind that elementary math is more than just arithmetic. Learning math is about reasoning and solving problems worth solving. Brainstorm activities and tasks that support deep, meaningful learning, and think about the questions and discussions that are essential to learning. You can also adapt the context of word problems in existing mathematics curriculum to match the theme of a STEM project.

Review math and science standards to better understand what is developmentally appropriate for the grade level of the children for whom the project is designed.

Consider how to connect with what the children are learning in school and the knowledge they already have. This should be done in tandem with the prior step. Finding math and science connections that align with grade-level expectations can be hard! For instance, suppose a science experiment allows third graders to investigate a phenomenon and collect data. It might be tempting to ask kids to find averages of the data they collect and make predictions. Even though the science topic may align with third-grade standards, third graders are just beginning to learn multiplication and early division—and measures of central tendency (e.g., mean, median, mode) first appear in the CCSSM in grade 6! The challenge of aligning a theme with grade-level standards in both math and science typically requires some toggling and creativity. Extending the same third-grade example, maybe children have recently learned about fractions (a big part of the third-grade math curriculum). Instead of finding averages of data collected, why not set up a situation that will yield some fraction data points that children can plot on a number line (CCSSM 3.NF.A.2)? Then represent multiple data points by making a line plot of fractional measures (CCSSM 3.MD.B.4). In this way, whatever third-grade science activity you had planned will also provide a context for learning appropriate third-grade math content.

Sometimes there isn't a perfect fit between math and science, even when the theme offers a really rich learning opportunity in one subject but nothing corresponds at grade level for the other subject. In this case, consider grade bands and how you could reinforce standards from prior grades or lay early foundations for learning standards that might not appear until next year. Also consider individual children's strengths and challenges as you decide what is appropriate.

Seek out technologies that capture children's attention, extend their understanding of math and/or science, and provide opportunities to develop technological literacy and expectations as described in the ISTE Standards for Students.

Often, the hardest part about matching technology learning opportunities is narrowing down your options. Start with resources from reputable sites, perhaps those connected with school curriculum materials, universities, or museums. Consider exploratory online applets, apps, educational games, and videos, and keep in mind how the technology resources you select actually support learning. Does watching a video count as technology if it is just someone lecturing to the child on a screen? Maybe, but there are probably much better options. On the other hand, if a video includes a really useful simulation and/or serves a clear educational purpose, perhaps it is the right resource for your needs. Also keep in mind that children's technology learning is about much more than passively accessing information with technology. Look for opportunities for kids to choose among technology options, create and reason with technology, or communicate and collaborate. And while technology can be used to facilitate quizzes or other more traditional assessments, why not let children document and reflect on their learning though more creative options involving technologies such as video creation, slide decks, or animations? The ISTE Standards for Students may also spark your imagination about the ways in which technology can be used to support math and science learning, while also providing options to learn about technology itself.

Explore projects that engage children in the engineering design process and apply or extend their learning about math, science, and technology.

Are there types of engineering or careers children can learn about in the context of the theme? Maybe you've seen a STEM design project on Pinterest or elsewhere that fits in with the theme of your project, or perhaps you remember something you built as a kid. You can draw inspiration from a number of sources, but keep in mind the following key features of engineering, especially at the elementary level: engineering applies math and science to solve problems, engineering involves a purposeful design process with iteration and reflection (not just endless trial and error), and building can be part of engineering but engineering is more than just building. Also be mindful that, although the engineering design process and scientific method have much in common, they are not the same thing. The scientific method focuses on posing a question and answering it through testing and experimentation; the engineering design process finds practical solutions to problems. Both are important, but providing children with opportunities to learn about both science and engineering can enrich STEM learning.

Brainstorm connections to other subject areas and media.

Children's books are always a good idea for advancing reading and literacy while exploring a topic more deeply. Writing can also be a fairly easy connection to make, particularly when you consider multimodal and multilingual opportunities for storytelling and expression. Then consider how you can connect the theme with social studies, art, music, PE, and computer science or robotics. Are there opportunities to extend learning about the topic through video games, movies, or television shows? Especially when it comes to managing the challenges of distance learning from home for elementary children, a well-designed mix of explicitly educational opportunities and potentially educational entertainment can increase the child's engagement and blur the line between learning and playing (so long as purposeful learning is still occurring!).

When designing for distance STEM learning, teachers must make decisions along the way about how to convey activities in an accessible, digital format. The activities you design within your projects might include tables or worksheets, often leveraging dynamic online documents (e.g., Google Docs or Microsoft 365) with downloadable options for offline use. For more hands-on activities, consider how students could document, share, discuss, and reflect on their learning in a distance environment. Distance schooling does not have to mean all learning happens while seated at a computer. On the contrary, the types of projects in this book encourage children to explore, experiment, and actively engage in offline activities that are thoughtfully paired with distance learning.

For families looking to balance more traditional distance schoolwork with active, project-based learning, these STEM projects may focus more on the offline activities, with online connections coming more from school curriculum. In fact, such motivations may completely change the order of steps for designing STEM projects. Families may begin with the math and/or science that children are learning in distance schooling, and from there identify themes for projects that support and enrich through integrated STEM learning. The goal of engaging children in meaningful learning remains the same.

In Conclusion

Designing STEM projects for elementary distance learning is not a one-size-fits-all endeavor. Teachers and families can draw from the projects in this book and the guidelines in this chapter to create rich, engaging activities that address grade-level standards while also connecting with other content areas in ways that interest and excite young children.

References

Bidwell, J. K. (1993, September). Humanize your classroom with the history of mathematics. *Mathematics Teacher, 86*(6), 461–64.

Carpenter, T. P., Fennema, E., & Franke, M. L. (1996). Cognitively guided instruction: A knowledge base for reform in primary mathematics instruction. *The Elementary School Journal, 97*(1), 3–20. https://doi.org/10.1086/461846

Carroll, M. (2019, March 14). Make: Projects. Scrappy Circuits. https://makezine.com/projects/scrappy-circuits

Duran, L. B. & Duran, E. (2004). The 5E Instructional Model: A learning cycle approach for inquiry-based science teaching. *Science Education Review, 3*(2) 49–58. https://files.eric.ed.gov/fulltext/EJ1058007.pdf

Franklin, C., Kader, G., Mewborn, D., Moreno, J., Peck, R., Perry, M., & Scheaffer, R. (2007). Guidelines for Assessment and Instruction in Statistics Education (GAISE) report: A pre-K–12 curriculum framework. American Statistical Association. http://www.professores.im-uff.mat.br/hjbortol/disciplinas/2012.2/esp00001/arquivos/gaise-1.pdf

Gravemeijer, K., Bowers, J. & Stephan, M. (2003, January). Supporting students' development of measuring conceptions: Analyzing students' learning in social context. *Journal for Research in Mathematics Education, 12.*

JCGM. (2008). International vocabulary of metrology–basic and general concepts and associated terms (VIVM3). Joint Committee for Guides in Metrology, 200. http://www.bipm.org/en/publications/guides/vim.html

Jones, P. S. (1957). The history of mathematics as a teaching tool. *The Mathematics Teacher, 50,* 59–64.

Karp, K. S., Bush, S. B., & Dougherty, B. J. (2019, May). Avoiding the ineffective keyword strategy. *Teaching Children Mathematics, 25*(7).

Mercer, N., Dawes, L., Wegerif, R., & Sams, C. (2004). Reasoning as a scientist: Ways of helping children to use language to learn science. *British Educational Research Journal, 30*(3), 359–377. https://doi.org/10.1080/01411920410001689689

Museum of Science, Boston. (2020). *The Engineering design process in action* [Video]. http://d7.eie.org/eie-curriculum/resources/engineering-design-process-action

National Council of Teachers of Mathematics. (2014). Principles to actions: Ensuring mathematical success for all.

O'Connell, J. & Groom, D. (2010). *Virtual worlds: Learning in a changing world*. ACER Press.

Pruitt, S. L. (2014, March 22). The Next Generation Science Standards: The features and challenges. *Journal of Science Teacher Education, 25,* 145–156. https://doi.org/10.1007/s10972-014-9385-0

Reys, B. J., Thomas, A., Tran, D., Newton, J., Kasmer, L. A., Teuscher, D., & Dingman, S. (Fall/Winter 2012–2013). State-level actions following adoption of Common Core State Standards for Mathematics. *NCSM Journal of Mathematics Leadership, 14*(2).

Rose, P. (2014, November 27). Achieving equitable quality education post-2015: Indicators to measure progress towards learning and equity. The Education and Development Forum (UKFIET). https://www.ukfiet.org/2014/achieving-equitable-quality-education-post-2015-indicators-to-measure-progress-towards-learning-and-equity

Sfard, A. (2001, March). There is more to discourse than meets the ears: Looking at thinking as communicating to learn more about mathematical learning. *Educational Studies in Mathematics, 46*(1), 13–57. https://doi.org/10.1023/A:1014097416157

Szilagyi, J., Clements, D.H., & Sarama, J. (2013, May). Young children's understandings of length measurement: Evaluating a learning trajectory. *Journal for Research in Mathematics Education, 44*(3), 581–620. http://dx.doi.org/10.5951/jresematheduc.44.3.0581

Xie, J. Z., Tarczy-Hornoch, K., Lin, J., Cotter, S. A., Torres, M., & Varma, R. (2014, April 3). Color vision deficiency in preschool children: The multi-ethnic pediatric eye disease study. *Ophthalmology, 121*(7), 1469–1474. https://doi.org/10.1016/j.ophtha.2014.01.018

Works Consulted

Ames, C. (1990). Motivation: What teachers need to know. *Teachers College Record, 91*(3), 409–421. pdfs.semanticscholar.org/1623/e9f4540535eaef691375127de7686145a616.pdf

Alderman, M. K. (2013). *Motivation for achievement: Possibilities for teaching and learning* (3rd ed.). Routledge.

Anderson, M., & Jiang, J. (2018, November 28). Teens' social media habits and experiences. *Pew Research Center.* pewinternet.org/2018/11/28/teens-social-media-habits-and-experiences

Baker, C. (2010, January). The impact of instructor immediacy and presence for online student affective learning, cognition, and motivation. *The Journal of Educators Online, 7*(1). files.eric.ed.gov/fulltext/EJ904072.pdf

Barrett, P., Zhang, Y., Moffat, J., & Kobbacy, K. (2013, January). A holistic, multi-level analysis identifying the impact of classroom design on pupils' learning. *Building and Environment, 59,* 678–689. https://doi.org/10.1016/j.buildenv.2012.09.016

Barrett, P., Davies, F. M., Zhang, Y., & Barrett, L. (2015, July). The impact of classroom design on pupils' learning: Final results of a holistic, multi-level analysis. *Building and Environment, 89,* 118–133. https://doi.org/10.1016/j.buildenv.2015.02.013

Boss, S., & Krauss, J. (2018). *Reinventing project-based learning: Your field guide to real-world projects in the digital age* (3rd ed.). ISTE.

Brophy, J. (2004). *Motivating students to learn* (2nd ed.). Lawrence Erlbaum Associates.

Casa-Todd, J. (2017). *Social LEADia: Moving students from digital citizenship to digital leadership.* Dave Burgess Consulting, Inc.

Curran, M. B.F.X., & Dee, C. (Eds.) (2019). *DigCitKids: Lessons learning side-by-side, to empower others around the world.* EduMatch.

Donally, J. (2018). *Learning transported: Augmented, virtual and mixed reality for all classrooms.* ISTE.

Gallup & NewSchools Venture Fund. (2019). Education technology use in schools: Student and educator perspectives. newschools.org/wp-content/uploads/2019/09/Gallup-Ed-Tech-Use-in-Schools-2.pdf

[GBH News]. (2013, December 6). *Raw video: Nelson Mandela visits Madison Park HS in Roxbury in 1990* [Video]. YouTube. youtube.com/watch?v=b66c6OkMZGw

Geng, S., Law, K. M. Y., & Niu, B. (2019, May 21). Investigating self-directed learning and technology readiness in blending learning environment. *International Journal of Educational Technology in Higher Education, 16(17).* https://doi.org/10.1186/s41239-019-0147-0

Gerstein, J. (2013, March 22). Schools are doing education 1.0; talking about doing education 2.0; when they should be planning education 3.0. *User Generated Education.* usergeneratededucation.wordpress.com/2013/03/22

Gura, M. (2016). *Make, learn, succeed: Building a culture of creativity in your school.* ISTE.

Highfill, L., Hilton, K., & Landis, S. (2016). *The HyperDoc handbook: Digital lesson design using Google apps.* Elevate Books Edu.

Kim, M., & Choi, D. (2018). Development of youth digital citizenship scale and implication for educational setting. *Educational Technology & Society, 21*(1), 155–171. jstor.org/stable/26273877

Kolb, L. (2017). *Learning first, technology second: The educator's guide to designing authentic lessons.* ISTE.

Krebs, D., & Zvi, G. (2015). *The genius hour guidebook: Fostering passion, wonder, and inquiry in the classroom.* Routledge.

Kulowiec, G. (2013, February 26). App smashing—from Greg. *EdTechTeacher*. edtechteacher.org/app-smashing-from-greg

LaGarde, J., & Hudgins, D. (2018). *Fact vs. fiction: Teaching critical thinking skills in the age of fake news*. ISTE.

Lindsay, J. (2016). *The global educator: Leveraging technology for collaborative learning and teaching*. ISTE.

Linklater, R. (Director). (2003). *School of rock* [Film]. Paramount Pictures.

Mahoney, J. L., Durlak, J. A., & Weissberg, R. P. (2018, November 26). An update on social and emotional learning outcome research. *Phi Delta Kappan, 100*(4), 18–23. https://doi.org/10.1177/0031721718815668

Mattson, K. (2017). *Digital citizenship in action: Empowering students to engage in online communities*. ISTE.

McGraw-Hill Education Applied Learning Sciences Team. (2017,November 13). Fostering social and emotional learning (SEL) through technology. *Medium*. medium.com/inspired-ideas-prek-12/fostering-social-emotional-learning-through-technology-8da6974e54bb

McNair, A. (2017). *Genius hour: Passion projects that ignite innovation and student inquiry*. Prufrock Press.

Papert, S. (1980). *Mindstorms: Children, computers, and powerful ideas*. Basic Books.

Papert, S. (2000). What's the big idea? Toward a pedagogy of idea power. *IBM Systems Journal, 39*(3&4), 720–729. llk.media.mit.edu/courses/readings/Papert-Big-Idea.pdf

Papert, S., & Harel, I. (1991). *Constructionism*. Ablex Publishing Corporation. papert.org/articles/SituatingConstructionism.html

Petersen, M. (2001). *Mathematical Harmonies*. https://amath.colorado.edu/pub/matlab/music/MathMusic.pdf

PwC. (2018). The talent challenge: Rebalancing skills for the digital age. pwc.com/gx/en/ceo-survey/2018/deep-dives/pwc-ceo-survey-talent.pdf

Ribble, M. (2015). *Digital citizenship in schools: Nine elements all students should know* (3rd ed.). ISTE.

Rideout, V., & Robb, M. B. (2018). Social media, social life: Teens reveal their experiences. Common Sense Media. commonsensemedia.org/sites/default/files/uploads/research/2018_cs_socialmediasociallife_executivesummary-final-release_3_lowres.pdf

Robinson, K. (n.d.). Ken Robinson quotes. BrainyQuote. BrainyQuote.com brainyquote.com/quotes/ken_robinson_561890

Rohde, M. (2012). *The sketchnote handbook: The illustrated guide to visual notetaking.* Peachpit Press.

Ryan, R. M., & Deci, E. L. (2000). Intrinsic and extrinsic motivations: Classic definitions and new directions. *Contemporary Educational Psychology, 25*(1), 54–67. https://doi.org/10.1006/ceps.1999.1020

Seymour Papert. (n.d.). papert.org

Sheninger, E. C. (2019). *Digital leadership: Changing paradigms for changing times.* Corwin.

Spencer, J., & Juliani, A. J. (2016). *Launch: Using design thinking to boost creativity and bring out the maker in every student.* Dave Burgess Consulting, Inc.

Thomas, S., Howard, N. R., & Schaffer, R. (2019). *Closing the gap: Digital equity strategies for the K–12 classroom.* ISTE.

Tucker, C. R., Wycoff, T., & Green, J. T. (2016). *Blended learning in action: A practical guide toward sustainable change.* Corwin.

Webb, N. L. (2014). Depth of knowledge for mathematics. In R.E. Slavin (Ed.) *Science, technology, & mathematics (STEM),* 22–25. Corwin. dx.doi.org/10.4135/9781483377544.n6

Wettrick, D. (2014). *Pure genius: Building a culture of innovation and taking 20% time to the next level.* Dave Burgess Consulting, Inc.

Whiteside, A. L. (2015). Introducing the social presence model to explore online and blended learning experiences [Doctoral dissertation]. *Online Learning Journal, 19*(2). olj.onlinelearningconsortium.org/index.php/olj/article/view/453

Van Malderen, G. (2019, July 22). 3 ways #EdTech is key to narrowing the educational achievement gap. *FE News.* fenews.co.uk/featured-article/32243

Vega, V., & Robb, M. B. (2019). The Common Sense census: Inside the 21st century classroom. Common Sense Media. commonsensemedia.org/sites/default/files/uploads/research/2019-educator-census-inside-the-21st-century-classroom_1.pdf

Zimmerman, E. (2019, September 13). How technology can improve digital citizenship in K–12. *EdTech.* edtechmagazine.com/k12/article/2019/09/how-technology-can-improve-digital-citizenship-k-12-perfcon

Index